MEDIA: SENSATION NOT TRUTH

MEDIA

Sensation Not Truth

S.C. Bhatt

GYAN PUBLISHING HOUSE
New Delhi-110002

MEDIA: SENSATION NOT TRUTH
(*Media, Press*)

Rs. 390

ISBN: 81-212-0818-1

Published in 2003 in India by
Gyan Publishing House
5, Ansari Road
New Delhi 110 002
Phones: 3261060, 3282060, Fax: 3285914
e-mail: gyanbook@vsnl.com
visit our website at: http://www.gyanbooks.com

Laser Typeset at Alphabet, Delhi
Printed at Mehra Offset Printers, Delhi

Contents

Contents

Preface

"Quit call to Modi, Parliament stalled" says the *Times of India* on April 16, 2002, the first day of the two houses as Parliament reconvened for the resumption of the Budget session. Apart from the banner heading, more than half the front page was occupied by the media's ire against the Gujarat Chief Minister. There was a sub-heading "Opp closes ranks for censure motion" and there was another item, bylined, "Allies unimpressed with BJP hardsell" and a cartoon. Considering nothing stirs in the paper without a mastermind directing the staff, the cartoon could have been prearranged. In any case, the edit page had plenty of anti-Modi material.

This is the kind of interest evinced in ousting Modi in which the paper had personal stake. It is of no concern to the media that Parliament was "stalled", as the *Times* said. A day wasted in the life of the 13th Parliament is a matter of no concern to the media. Many more days are thus wasted and the journalistic fraternity is the least concerned.

The media, may it be the print variety, the electronic media, or the TV channels, all are interested in sensationalising the events, whether it is Parliament or the events outside. The Gujarat situation is far from good but it does not behove a paper which is easily the best in the country and the most successful and well-circulated at that, to take a personal interest in the matter as though its very fate depended on the Modi ouster. Woe begotten is the paper which looks upon the resignation in this way.

This book with appropriate quotes from the media itself deals with the question of the media prefering sensation to truth. The houses of Parliament are supposed to be rocked if a single member shouts and enters the well. The news is not presented in the form in which the readers are accustomed to, but in the manner which the paper fancies. What the papers prefer and often go in for is the series of features in which the first para tells us nothing. But for the heading the news often becomes a casualty. The format is thus changed as colour is a must and the entire printing technology is changed beyond recognition. Much of the change is to be welcomed and has been accepted by the readers but the papers are taking too much liberty with the readers' preferences. News has to be presented as it is, if regard for truth and credibility are the criterion.

The English papers dictate terms to the Indian language papers which to a large extent depend on the news agencies which are themselves catering to the English media and indulge in competition for the sake of it and out of necessity at times. The source having been "polluted", as it is there is not much that can be done even if the editors want it. However, it is clarified that the English media, and a large section of it, indulge in the "sensation, not truth" approach.

The electronic media, meaning the TV channels, are becoming vehicles of news. What the TV medium provides is entertainment and when the breadwinner of the family returns home in the evening he immediately sits in front of the TV set and surfs channels. As he does so, he is inclined to his favourite news channel and this raises the question whether the newspapers are becoming redundant because the main person of the family watches the news on his TV channel and this is likely to serve the purpose of getting news unifluencd by anybody. There is no question of disposing of the TV set. Thus, the newspaper is in the danger of being considered dispensable.

This study was undertaken spread over three years, because the writer felt that the media had embarked on a deliberate exercise of sensationalising news which was borne out by the study. There are a sections of the media which are truthful but their number is limited. But the sections of the media which are not bound by the old discipline are much larger. News is so sensationalised by media as if the world was coming to an end. People tend to forget that their newspaper had predicted the gory things, but a time may come when the unforgetful habit is overtaken in the end and people stop buying the paper. It is clarified that writer has no commitment to any ideology or alliance. But truth requires that some things need be told in a particular manner and there is scope for a statement of facts.

The media like individual prefer some parties and factions to others and we have no quarrel with that approach but the approach has to be straight and not crooked. When the reporter comments from the very start and his report becomes an exercise in comments it is inevitable that the preferences become evident. Certain level of comment is inescapable but there is a limit beyond which a reporter should not go.

The media's preference for conflict as the source of all news is recognised but what is objected to, is the fondness for sensation rather than truth.

S.C. Bhatt

One

News and its Manifestation

Media freedom, the wider meaning of press freedom, upheld by the highest court, the Supreme Court of India, is part of our democratic system. It is one of the pillars on which the entire superstructure of India is based. What the media are expected to bring to their audience, through the daily medium of the print media or the instant medium of the electronic variety, is news based on facts. The news and its interpretation is the staple diet of the media. There is absolutely no question of anybody putting any restraint or check on the media on this account as it is this, their primary task.

But it casts several obligations on the media, one of the major of which is the duty and the need to check. The facts have to be checked and while some fanfare is justified, the source must be clearly indicated if not identified. The need to play up conflict is well recognised, because conflict becomes the mother of almost all news stories, as in fiction, novel, short story, film or TV serials. But that does not mean that all news should be sensationalised. Facts should be presented in as much of an unvarnished condition as possible. There is plenty happening as it is, but it may be necessary sometimes to present facts in a manner likely to attract the readers or viewer's attention. But when this is overdone and made into a habit, the truth goes out and sensation takes over.

It is recognised that the various media have to portray the good with the bad. What the media have to note is that the bad becomes obligatory on them to depict to the exclusion of the good. Most media, however, portray the bad because they believe that it sells in this competitive world, as all successful media have to operate. Without competition there is no progress as some pampered media have found out. But competition should not mean that the taken notion about the bad always selling should be accepted as a 'mantra' and ruthlessly followed.

As stated before, there is need and a media obligation to check out the facts. If the story is played up, one has to tender an abject apology because the need to check has been overlooked and marginalised. Readers would do well to scan the author's book, *Broadcast Journalism: Basic Principles*[1]. It deals extensively with the problem of the nature of news and the need of checking. An example is quoted of an agency correspondent who on seeing a fire wanted to interview the town's fire officer when there was just no need. He was so keen on checking his facts.

The ignoring of the basic requirement of checking results sometimes results in an abject apology as in the case of a senior correspondent of the *Times of India*, the leading newspaper of India. Siddarth Varadarajan, the deputy chief of the paper's news bureau, said in a signed story on May, 23, 2001, "MEA was right after all". A senior person with another prestigious newspaper, the *Hindu* of Chennai which has spread to several cities, including the national capital, Delhi, was guilty of the same thing. Harish Khare, who was earlier with the *Times* and held important positions, including the editorship of the Ahmedabad edition of the paper, said in the *Hindu* on May 23 in a bylined story "Ceasefire Extension Imminent". That was in the context of the Ceasefire unilaterally imposed in Jammu and Kashmir by Prime Minister Atal Bihari Vajpayee in November 2000 and extended from time to time. The question in May 2001 was whether there would be an extension of the unilateral ceasefire.

Surprisingly, the very next day, on May 24, again in a bylined story, the eminent journalist, without so much as batting an eyelid said, "Vajpayee Invites Musharraf" *in bold types and then in small types* "Ceasefire off...." There was apparently no attempt at checking the earlier story. True, if Khare had tried to get confirmation he would have met with a polite "sorry, no comments" but the crux of the matter is that the eminent journalist preferred to proclaim to the whole world that the Indian government would definitely extend the ceasefire and with the same elan he reported exactly the opposite story the next day. He mentioned no attempt on his part to contact the sources and hinted at no such thing that it was not confirmed or he got a rebuff[2].

The media should care for confirmation if they lay some importance to their credibility. While the *Times of India* doggedly pursues its pet theory that India came off badly at the July summit at Agra, its star correspondent, Siddharth Varadarajan, thinks no end of himself but had to eat a humble pie and acknowledge that he erred in the EA ministry story, as we saw. The paper, however, loses no opportunity to tell us that it carries only factual reports. It uses a lot of embroidery in doing so and often errs as it did on the story concerned. Events move with such lightning speed that if you insisted on the readers accepting your statement as gospel truth you not only look foolish and may have no new statement to make.

With the new trend of playing up the sensational to the exclusion of a truthful account of what happened we have to take account also of the vast technological changes, both in the print media as well as the electronic media. Colour is a must in every daily or weekly newspaper, even for those living on the edge of survival and, in fact, the meanest newspaper. The reader today has come to expect from his daily paper that it will bring to him a colourful account, of not only words but pictures, of the most notable event of the day. This has been facilitated by the revolution in printing and with it goes the overgrown size of the daily newspaper. Gone are the days when the reader, the most busy urban reader and the village dweller who can afford to buy his own paper, would be content with a four page or six page paper. Now he wants a larger paper, with plenty of coloured photographs, easy to read, layout, attractive to the eyes and readable pages and readable columns.

How one wishes that the media also paid as much attention to their contents as to the get-up, the sizes of the papers the coloured photographs which go to adorn the pages, including the additional pages. What one notices how is a complete change in most of the daily papers in the presentation of news. In the old days, the readers laid much store and expected the papers to emphasise the Five W's and the intro without which the sub-editor in charge of the edition would not pass the deskman's copy. The intro, short for introduction, generally contained the most important part of the story and the heading was usually contained in the intro.

What now happens is a complete reversal. The story begins with a generalisation which is irrelevant in many cases and sometimes even wrong and often the heading saves the story. The heading gives you the news and the belief that most busy readers scan only the headings of their paper is strengthened by this practise often resorted to by the dailies. What is important to note is that often such stories appear on the front pages of a newspaper whereas in the past they were carried on an inside page as a feature. It is good to find that many news stories are featurised in this manner but the distinction between a news story and a feature should be maintained.

In the old days, many Indian language papers carried instead of the intro a long dissertation and only the heading told you what the story contained and the reader would if he was interested read the entire story. This pattern is still followed by some Indian language dailies and this is further strengthened by some sophisticated papers following the practice.

The old newsmen insist on their intro. For example, if a Chief Minister or the Prime Minister sacks one of his ministers the old-style story is somewhat like this: "The Chief Minister (of a certain state) today sacked his Minister (followed by his name and portfolio) for (whatever his crime or fault may be)". But now the situation is different. First of all, the privilege of doing the story, in fact all important stories, lies in Delhi usually by the all-knowing Political correspondent (Usually somebody like Siddarth Varadarajan, not he in particular or those operating under similar titles. Time was when New Delhi scribes place their stories even in remote places like Longju in Arunachal Pradesh at the height of the India-China tension which was followed by China's regular invasion in 1962. Now the trend is the other way about. The Center is not worried by the story being lodged in Delhi itself. The story begins with comments and interpretation, as is the present style, and the correspondent does not wait for the main story to sink in the minds of his readers before he offers his comments and interpretation.

This routine is followed in most cases and sometimes the regional correspondent's presence is acknowledged by such stories as "Our Lucknow correspondent adds or the Chandigarh correspondent has this to say". The presumption is that the New Delhi man is too learned and has some special knowledge of every state. There is no question of the special right of these gentlemen to offer comments on happenings in states being taken away. The reader has no option but to gulp the New Delhi datelined story with his morning cup of tea. Technological changes are also coming to the aid of the New Delhi man as he has at his disposal the long distance phone. The management of the paper has to be convinced but that is no problem considering the competition. The management has, however, to worry why the paper has to have a highly paid regional correspondent if the New Delhi correspondent can handle his job as well. However, if he has any doubts on this score he better leave this to himself. The Political correspondent is supposed to be so powerful that the management can be sacked at his instance.

Then an aspect of the technological change is as stated reflected in the size of the papers. In the good old days, the presence of such characters as film stars, ad agency whizkids and models was indirectly acknowledged by including this, in the form of interviews in the regular pages of newspapers. I still remember the interview which the *Times of India* had with Amitabh Bachchan, who had the status of a superstar even in those days and who advanced the silly argument on behalf of Bollywood to defend violence in films that the cinema used to make sauce instead of real blood. He forgot that what was relevant to the paying audience that the person, usually the villain's henchmen or the villain himself and sometimes an innocent person, was actually "killed".

The other interview was with Ajay Deavgan, who promised much during those days but is yet to attain stardom. He made an honest confession that he had "no time" to read a daily paper. Now the proper vehicle for carrying such stuff is the additional pages like *HT City* or *Delhi Times*. They carry such items like cinema gossip, or the doings of cinema stars, no matter what their status is, on their visits to Delhi, which is quite often, or places like Lucknow or Ahmedabad. It is a sign of the declining status of the politicians that people like Amar Singh, the omnipresent general secretary of the Samajwadi party, has to identify himself with people like Bachchan and mix with all kinds of stars and starlets to get political clout. The cinema stories which now dominate the additional pages of the dailies are the legitimate stuff which go to adorn the pages of the cinema mags, which is short for magazines. They have mistakenly moved on to what they regard as a higher plane.

But the pages are hard to fill even with the cinemas stuff so the models, fashion experts and advertisement people come in, in fact, all with some clout are welcome to occupy some space in the additional pages. The ad agency people extract their price because of the favours they do to the papers. In the process of filling up their pages the papers do not forget which side their bread is buttered. The newspapers are also conscious of the need to increase their circulation and resort to the usual and some unusual gimmicks. They produce any number of special supplements and circulate copies of their papers free to many sections of readers. After a time, when the papers think that enough is enough they withdraw the free supply but take care to ensure that the readers in question get the paper.

Circulation gimmicks are well known but the pretence which the papers employ is sometimes amazing. Some of them have the websites of their own and interview the supposed celebrity there. Readers are supposed to log on to these sites, more than once a day. All papers care for the spread of AIDS and sex before marriage but encourage through the additional pages and otherwise the permissive approach recklessly[3]. The *Times of India* was the first paper in the capital (and elsewhere to have additional pages. What the *Times* does today the *Hindustan Times*, the oldest daily of Delhi, does tomorrow without admitting it. The oldest paper employed bright people, as did the one before it, to prepare these pages and also to contribute to their regular columns. The papers employed the tactics to enhance their acceptability and management proved its superiority over the editorial. The editor was useful if only he raised the circulation of the paper. In such a situation, no wonder the editors are often forgotten and seldom remembered.

The role of the media is the constant topic of discussion by the VVIP, specially if the occasion demands it. This is repeatedly referred to in the media themselves, particularly the print media and occasional and regular contributors to the media. The Vice President of India, who presides over the Rajya Sabha, the upper house of Parliament, as part of his functions, had bitter things to say at a conference on the performance of the media in parliamentary coverage. To quote his words, Krishan Kant said: "An impression was growing among parliamentarians that the media was interested *only in reporting what was sensational*." (Emphasis added)[4]. The Vice President went on to elaborate his succinct observation to highlight the playing up of the disorderly and unseemly conduct of some members and downplaying the sober, serious and thoughtful contribution of others.

Interestingly, Mani Shankar Aiyar, a Congress MP, in the more noisy lower house, the Lok Sabha, also known to be a trenchant critic of the present set-up but a friend of the media, had important observations to make of the manner in which the media covered parliamentary proceedings. Writing in the *Hindustan Times* on the ban on MPs entering the well of the house, with the automatic suspension for seven days and all parties agreeing to it, with the exception of the Samajwadi party, he made drastic comments on the habit of the media to openly prefer the *sensational and ignore the serious debates*. (Emphasis added).

Mani Shankar Aiyar said in the paper[5]: "The root cause of paulitics as *hangama* (the spelling coined by Aiyar himself) is the collaboration *(millibhagat* is the *pauliticswallahs*' favoured phase for this) between the media and the disrupters. If word leaks out that the well is to be invaded, the press gallery is immediately invaded, journos (journalists) jostling each other to get a better, more personalised view of the goings-on so that the next morning lends their special brand of colour to the rich text box item on page one carrying their by-line, which is the whole object of their professional ambitions. If on the other hand word leaks out that there is going to be an actual debate, and that too on a serious national issue, and that too stretching into the night, the press gallery takes to its heels......"

In his article, Aiyar also records from memory that on December 22, 1993, when Lok Sabha was discussing population policy not a single pressman or woman was present and a record of sorts was set up. This observation is important because it comes straight from the horse's mouth it comes from a friend of the media and it comes out of the pen of a present set-up's enemy number one. It highlights the media's approach of glorifying the sensational to the exclusion of truthful and the relevant. So much importance is laid in the media on the entering of the well by some irate members that even the papers and the bulletins of All India Radio play it up.

Finally the Speaker of the Lok Sabha, G.M.C. Balayogi, got sick of the habit of some opposition members to walk into the well of the house and convened a meeting of the party heads who readily or reluctantly agreed to the ban on the entering the well with penalty of suspension from the house for seven days. It is mystery why the Speaker did not use his powers to regulate the proceedings of the house earlier. Perhaps he was reluctant to use his powers and that helped the opposition members and the media in the press gallery who were in a kind of collaboration or conspiracy, as alleged by no less a member than Mani Shankar Aiyar.

The role of the media, in any case, is quite clear and certainly not a noble one. They neither condemned those members who entered the well of the house nor indeed the role of the Congress party in repeatedly disrupting the proceedings of the two houses on some pretext or another. In one session it is one thing, in another it is something else. The media's silence on the opposition members behaviour is Worth noting. The total absence of observation except by a paper or two, is a reflection on the question of parliamentary coverage. The media could have played a more positive role by pointing out that the MPs were not within their rights in what they did and they should have behaved better. In doing so, they would have to work a lot harder and not report from day to day the disruption of the proceedings. What Aiyar says is of great relevance. His support comes from the media factions themselves. The media found it easy to find that their copy got first rate coverage when they highlighted the entry into the well or the Congress party MPs holding up proceedings.

The media's silence on the strikes and *bandh* calls is equally intriguing. They prefer to contradict the government version and say that the strike was totally successful but never go deep into the question why the strike was essential in the first instance. When the Kerala High Court banned the *bandh* calls frequently given by the CPIM or its labour unions, they kept quiet but gave more than enough publicity to the CPIM's flimsy excuses when that party chose to comment on the Kerala judgement. They do not relish the situation where they are in conflict with the trade unions under whatever colour they may be going. Why annoy the trade unions, let us bother about the national loss and things like that, seems to be the media's approach. That the notice of the strike was given or not is not their concern.

They regret, on the one hand, their nation's fate but do not care to fight the evil. They perform only one duty, that of reporting the facts as they see them. They ignore that in their editorial comments they are expected to bring out the nation's loss because of the strike or the *bandh*.

The freedom that the media enjoy, to report the "facts" as they perceive them, is the gift of the BJP-led NDA government which is hardly acknowledged and never appreciated by the media. There is more media freedom under the rule of NDA government than under any previous Congress regime or even under two United Front governments in 1996 and 1997. There are not many laws which circumscribe the press and the electronic media. But the Congress regimes were notorious for *restaurants which* they put in the form of arm-twisting and other unpublicised methods. It is well known that the governments around the world have special departments to manage the press which term includes the electronic media also. The NDA government also has such machinery but it is known to function with due regard to the rights of the media. In any case, the media has come to regard and jealously guard the hard-won freedom and, rightly, want to protect their rights. This is welcome as it goes but we expect that the duties should be equally projected and protected as rights are. But the human tendency is to keep what suits it and forget about the rest. The media, therefore, likes to forget about its duty to project what is truthful and prefer sensation. Even, those projecting the official point of view indulge in exaggeration and provocation to satisfy themselves and their conscience. Such is the sorry state of affairs.

The Prime Minister Atal Bihari[6] Vajpayee, in his address to the World Congress and 50th General Assembly of the International Press Institute (IPI) in New Delhi, spoke of the need to enhance the credibility of the media through self-monitoring, self-regulation and where necessary through self-censorship. He was clear that the media should be totally free. While this should be so under all circumstances, the media should be accountable to the same extent as they expect the government, political parties businesses and private individuals to be accountable. Alas, the media are not so accountable. The print media, as well as the electronic media, while jealously guarding its citadel, are ready to jump at the slightest opportunity and lambast the government and its numerous agencies. The media, while enjoying freedom, wants nobody to look into its domain.

There prevailing mood is such that the media take their freedom for granted while they do not assume any responsibility so far even as the country is concerned. If tomorrow Pakistan was to attack India (assuming for argument's sake), the media will suffer at Pakistan's hands and even the *Times of India* which is more concerned with Pakistan is made to subserve the military dictator's purpose.

The press freedom will be the first casualty under the Pakistani government. The media will suffer under foreign yoke as will all other sections of society. The media are fully justified and within their rights to warn the government of the consequences of its policy but they are certainly not expected to favour Pakistan as some of the media are doing. When the Indian media quote, for example, Maj. Gen., Rashid, the Pakistan military ruler's press aide, one is tempted to laugh, at the total innocence of the media because he is widely known to exaggerate and make claims contrary to facts.

The media should not assume aloofness when it comes to dealing with India's hostile neighbours. This is not to suggest that they should deliberately colour their judgment and assume a hostile pose, but certainly not behave as though nothing of importance has happened. Unfortunately, some Muslims assume a contrary role and do not mind to flay their own government when it is in conflict with Pakistan. Instances of this attitude can be cited innumerable times, in the form of letters to the editor and statements to the press. When this attitude of criticism is attacked, some media flay the so-called anti-liberal approach and lack of secularism. The original lack of secularism is not invoked and that angers the people more.

We are opposed to the FDI investment in the print media and more so any foreign control of the print media. But do we realise that already the electronic media are invaded by foreigners. The examples are all there for us to see and should not be pointed out. The media are prone to point out when the authorities take action against a foreign channel or when they violate some standing rule and make a minor hullabaloo. Some of the respectable media are in that category. The foreign channels are subtly exercising their control. They are primarily interested in making money but in so doing they are influencing the viewers and the permissive attitude displayed by the print media who oppose otherwise the entry of FDIs, not to mention investment of more injurious kind. The leading papers look askance at the national channel of Doordarshan and loose no opportunity of sniping at the DD programmes in season and out of season. They do not realise that they are opposed to free foreigners in their print media although they are always lauding the foreign TV channels operating in India.

As it is, several DD programmes are taken over by the other channels, like Junoon, Kundali (latest example), Itihas, Swabhiman and others. One of the leading superstars of the Hindi screen, Shah Rukh Khan, was first exposed by DD and now he is not prepared to even acknowledge it. There are others not even equally famous. Many are faults of DD but not the ones pointed out by the media.

Some of the print media themselves carry, as pointed out earlier, that the columns criticising the approach of the media in playing up servile attitude of theirs in running after celebrities. Amrita Shah, a regular columnist of the *Indian Express,* which with it several Hindi and other Indian language papers and its extensive network is a true all-India paper, the only paper to acquire that status, complains in one of her columns that the media run after the celebrities. She also complains that the media does not care for the real and well-deserved academicians. She pointed out that it was futile to protect against this attitude[7]. Incidentally the *Indian Express* is very particular about the media freedom as it perceives it. It carried the Amrita Shah column all the same because it claims to uphold the views of its columnists, without supporting the same.

"Trial by Media the Tragedy of Devayani Rana" was

the heading of a specially contributed article by one Pooja Kothari, on the fate of the Nepali woman whom the Crown Prince wanted to marry before he killed his parents and others including himself. The paper was the *Times of India*[8]. The same paper was also the recipient of a number of refutations to some of which the correspondents concerned replied and some others were published without any refutation, obviously admissions. The *Indian Express* also carried a number of such refutations. It is the duty of all decent papers to carry letters written by individuals speaking on behalf of their organisations and agencies but the frequency of such refutations shows that there is not enough check and the correspondents rely on flimsy data, often an individual having a grouse against the organisation, and do not care to ask the agency or organisation what they have to say on the subject[9]. Often, the rivalry comes out. For example, the *Hindustan Times*, in an editorial on February 24, 2001 described the writings in the *Times of India* on the Balco deal, without naming the rival, as coming out of an "ill - informed section of the press". The *Times* carried on a campaign, one of the many the paper had, against the deal and it only ceased when the Supreme Court unequivocally upheld the deal. The *Times*, for instance, carried an article by one of its correspondents, "Cat among the Pigeons" to which it must have received many letters of protests from its readers. The paper often does not publish many letters, for example, when it carried the story that the *Al Zajeera*, of Qatar, was the only source of independent news whereas it was only one pro-Osama source which required to be compared with the lot coming out of Afghanistan which the paper itself published.

Coming to the "Cat among the Pigeons" story the paper had to publish L.D. Bhatia's article who wrote: "of all the

Indian papers that went out of their way to create unnecessary hype and hoopla over the (Pakistani) general's visit, the *Times of India* led the way in lionising and glorifying the general. The paper found new virtues is the man in the uniform. Its chief editor went to Islamabad to interview the self-appointed President and the interview was splashed prominently.... It is amusing to find that the paper is telling the readers now that the Indian media was taken for a ride by the Pakistani President.....". The article "Cat among the Pigeons" was published by the paper on July 24, 2001 and Bhatia's letter a few days thereafter.

That the Indians, or a section of the media, are down on India is testified by a number of foreigners. Writing in the *Vidura*, the Journal of the Press Institute of India, the then (London) *Times* correspondent, Christopher Thomas, said: "Britain is one of the world's most self-deprecating countries but India takes the lead in beating itself up. If Indians are down on India, what can the foreigners do?" The latter was in defence of the foreign correspondents known tendency to exaggerate and even falsify developments in India by reading the material in the Indian English language press who consider themselves as the custodians of liberalism and secularism. The foreign correspondents cannot absolve themselves of the charge of anti-Indian bias although the *London Times* correspondents comments are relevant.

The comments are supported by Francois Gautier, who regularly contributes to *The Indian Express*. He is a Frenchman who is a friend of India and who points out many failures on the part of India and Indians in a pleasant manner but their successes as well. He said: "Indians love turning themselves down. It is particularly true of the intelligencia, the intellectuals, the upper classes and the media. This is unfortunately a legacy of the colonial era." The paper headlined the article 'Indians a self-deprecating lot'[10]. The French correspondent had made the same point in his earlier articles also. It will neither be the last tie. But as the Agra summit showed, a number of journalists of the important media, which influence intellectuals, the tendency of the Indian media continues to be self-deprecatory. Exceptions also are, however, bound in the form of Bhatia.

The Indian Express often imitating foreign journals while giving complete sentences as headings, also makes fun of the Defence Minister George Fernandes who has made more than 20 trips to Siachen which was not visited even once by some of his predecessors. It stopped doing so when someone pointed out that calling him the loose cannon was yellow journalism. For all the liberty enjoyed by the print media, they do not like to be called the yellow press. But look at the sports headings of the paper. "Flannel misfits comfortable in pyjamas" *The Indian Express* said of the visiting Indian cricket team to Zimbabwe who won the first test and the heading was wrong to call the players as "flannel misfits". They won all the matches of the one-dayer variety except the final, hence the heading was wined[11].

Speaking of refutations, *The Indian Express* takes the cake when it accused[12] the national carrier, Air India, of removing all copies of the paper from Prime Minister Vajpayee's plane when he was going to Mauritius and it promptly apologised the next day in the following words: "AI's clarification: New Delhi: Reacting to the report published in the *Indian Express* on Saturday that Air India pulled out all copies of the paper from the PM's flight to Mauritius an Air India spokesman said the newspaper didn't reach the airport in time. The newspaper had carried a report on the pilots' blackmail. ENS" The reading should have been "The newspaper didn't reach the airport in time" instead of the bland AI Clarification. The media because of the freedom they enjoy can write anything but they cannot ensure the copies of the paper reaching that airport on time.

When the *Times of India* published[13] a report that Advani's men were guilty of snooping in the Liberhan Commission the very next day it had to publish a contradiction in the following words: "With reference to your report' Advani's men do some snooping' by Akshaya Mukul, the Liberhan Ayodhya Commission of Inquiry is an independent judicial body and is not under any ministry or person. Neither has the ministry of Home Affairs nor has any other person interfered with the working of the commission.... ". Incidentally Akshaya Mukul is one of the two correspondents imported from its rival, the *Hindustan Times*, for their special 'exercises' in such matters and has come in for comments on some occasions besides the Liberhan Commission. The Commission has been given many extensions and is expected to submit its report on the Babri mosque demolition which took place in December 1992.

There has been unremitting propaganda against HRD ministry and the Minister of the Vajpayee government inspired by the Leftists. There is little doubt that the man who heads the ministry, Murli Manohar Joshi, is a known BJP man having been President of the party and is known to put a red mark on his forehead, an anatheme to many a journalist, who are generally devotees of the bottle. He is supposed to be an RSS man. Let the media attack him on facts, not on Communist propaganda. If any facts come to light, it is the media's duty to publish them or air them on TV, but an *a priori* assumption that anything done by Joshi must be assumed to be saffron in content is a mistake on the part of the media.

One of the wrong assumptions is that the ICHR (Indian Council of Historical Research), which comes under the purview of the HRD ministry, was interfered with by Joshi. 'Leftists' misused ICHR: Chairman' was the heading of a story in the *Times of India* in which the newly appointed Chairman, Prof. M.G.S. Narayanan, an acknowledged history scholar, said that the media had swallowed the Leftist propaganda and attacked the ICHR in the past (nearly four years). The ICHR was dominated, Under the united Front and Congress rule, by well known Communists, who are also card-holders, like Irfan Habib and Romilla Thapar. "In the past", said Prof. Narayanan: "They the media never mentioned that the ICHR was used as an instrument by the so called Leftist historians for the benefit of their parties unscrupulously". He said that the journalists must have been totally ignorant of what happened before.

He should have added that the journalists were not history scholars or historians and still proceeded to attack Joshi under Communist inspiration.

Apparently *The Times* man went to the new chairman hoping that he would attack Joshi or tell him of the difficulties that he experienced under Joshi's hated regime. In any case, we are grateful to the paper for small mercies. It is too much to hope that it would help the paper to correct its past mistakes and in fact in February 2001 the Executive Editor of the paper, Dileep Padgaonkar, went to Patna in expectation of Laloo Prasad Yadav holding a big rally and came out with a story in which he compared Laloo with Gandhi himself ! "Laloo can be Gandhi Baba" said the *Times of India's* chief man hoping that Laloo's rally that Sunday would be something which the people of Bihar and of Patna would long remember. It is one of the print media's known tricks to do a story on the main character on the eve of a major event when the media are looking for favours and even otherwise.

Fortunately for the people of Bihar and unfortunately for *The Times* the rally flopped. The entire Patna press was unanimous about it including *The Times* which seemed to care more for its own credibility than the prestige of its chief editorial man. The rally, styled by Laloo as *"Desh bachao"* rally, did not even turn out as *"Laloo Bachao"*, much less Laloo turning into Gandhi Baba, as *The Times* had hoped. Laloo made no bones about who rules the unfortunate state of Bihar. Although he installed his semiliterate wife Rabri Devi when he was about to be taken to jail in July 1997 in the more than a billion rupee scandal when Laloo was not only Chief Minister but also the Finance Minister when allegedly no animal husbandry feed was purchased.

That Laloo is responsible for most of the ills of the state is known to every Bihari. The people of the state are intelligent and hard working. Nobody but Laloo would be taken in by Dileep Padgaonkar's story "Can Laloo play Gandhi Baba to Bihar" because the intelligent resident of the state knows that Laloo is guilty of the worst crimes, and is responsible for the total failure of the law and order machinery in the state. If the top man of the paper could do this to the paper and its readers, would Siddharth Varadarajan be found wanting in exploiting the paper's position? By virtue of his position and the special powers he exercises he called the Taliban regime' when in February 2001 they demolished the Buddha statues at Bamiyan' as not being taken seriously by the world and excused it of the worst crime against humanity on that ground. Can anyone indulge in a crime like this on the pretext that the world is not taking it seriously?

The Times is well managed, is in an expansive mood,

employs a large number of reporters to bring you all the stories which you would like to read. The paper is indeed readable and it would take some time to complete it. It is by far the most readable paper in India and adds new features constantly. But is it justified in taking the readers for granted when Dileep Padgaonkar and Siddharth Varadarajan did a story, ostensibly from Patna from New Delhi and called Laloo Gandhi, and Siddharth before going to Afghanistan justifiying the demolition of the Bamiyan statues?

When the ace correspondent went to Afghanistan he found a completely different picture. He could do little to salvage the situation and instead found a totally hated regime. The reports after the destruction of the Taliban regime pleased the people of Afghanistan after the Americans and the Northern Alliance succeeded in their mission.

The Editor of the *Hindustan Times*, Vir Sanghvi, could be accused of many things but he came out strongly against the use of prostitutes by the Tehelka team in their quest, as they say, of the defence ministry uncovering the corruption story. That defence ministry, with the three armed force wings in its train, was raking of corruption goes without saying and the Tehelka team should not have to go to those limits if uncovering corruption was their only object. However, the real test of a newspaper comes when it must take a stand on major issues before the nation. Editorially, the *Times of India* refused to take a stand whether the Tehelka should or should not have employed prostitutes as the *Hindustan Times* editor had done. It did so finally in a wishy-washy manner on September 3, 2001, a week and a day after the editor of a rival paper had done. In fact, there is no dearth of critics when the Tehelka team used hidden cameras as a device to attract witnesses to tell the truth.

The relevance of Gandhi is called in such cases but the plain fact is that Gandhiji did not approve at all of impure means being employed to achieve some "dignified" pure ends. To Gandhiji the means mattered always. Even on the Quit India movement Gandhiji thought of writing a letter to the British government in India to plead with them to quit their Indian empire before the British rulers struck in the early morning of August 9, 1942 and arrested Gandhiji and the Congress Working Committee members before they could carry out their plans. In other words, Gandhiji not only believed in the purity of means but actually practised it to the hilt.

This comes naturally to those who prefer sensation to truth. Whenever the choice confronts the media, they opt for the easy course and give many justifications and excuses for their preference. That will be put down by all thinking men as ends justify means holding the Gandhian analogy to ransom but there is a section of the media which justifies their preference on flimsy grounds and distorts Gandhiji in the process. The same attitude prevails in the larger context. For example, Mamata Banerjee was not asked why she rejoined the National Democratic. Alliance (NDA) in August 2001 when she had been loudest in demanding the resignation of George Fernandes in March that year. So did the PMK of Tamil Nadu which had abandoned the NDA in March that year. It must be said to the credit of the PMK that they had not asked for the resignation of the Defence Minister. The media play up demands by the CPIM to be followed by the Congress party in demanding the resignation of the Defence Minister on Coffins ordered by the Defence Ministry for the Kargil heroes Coffin scam to which the CAG (Comptroller and Auditor General) has drawn attention.

The plain fact is that NDA has displayed unexpected solidity and solidarity and Vajpayee's position seems unchallenged despite the BJP being in a minority. So, the opposition parties challenge the government and demand the resignation of this ministery and that and the media are ready to play on this allegation. Then there is astrology and Vedic mathematics introduced under the UGC (University Grants Commission) programme. Astrology is something to which the media pay homage by carrying columns daily and weekly forecasts of what the stars hold in store for you, but when the UGC introduces it as a subject for teaching in the universities the media, which, as always, means a section of it, object. This double role suits the media and it also lays them open to a charge, of not being consistent in their attitude. And the peculiarity of it all was that the West Bengal Chief Minister, Buddhadeb Bhattacharjee called a conference of all chief ministers to oppose the action of the UGC, there was absence of the Telugu Desam Chief Minister, N. Chandrababu Naidu, and the then Chief Minister of Tamil Nadu, J. Jayalalithaa (spelling as ordained by her) both of whom the media had predicted would attend.

In fact, almost all dailies, with a few honourable exceptions, regularly publish the weekly forecasts on pure astrological grounds (some even publish the daily forecasts) while they stealthily object to the UGC action. The leading campaigner publishes the column of a Parsi astrologer which he sometimes calls "Ganesha Speaks", making a mockery of astrology and all things connected with it, because to the absurdity of a Parsi upholding a Hindu God. The media are doing it for they wish to cater to the human frailty but they gaily criticise Murli Manohar Joshi and the UGC for putting the science of astrology, as the latter call it, in the curriculum of the Universities.

It would be interesting to recall that the *Illustrated Weekly of India*, a *Times of India* group publication now defunct, went to the extent of calling up leading astrologers to have their say when electoral interest was high as to who would be Prime Minister in May 1991 when elections were held to the Lok Sabha. The astrologers forecast, almost unanimously that Rajiv Gandhi would be the next Prime Minister while he was assassinated even as they were forecasting his elevation once again. V.P. Singh who had ruled for a year was a failure and Chandra Shekhar, who was allowed to rule for a few months thanks to the Congress party, was even a greater failure. The BJP, which now rules the country along with the NDA, was not much in the picture and the Left, the media know, makes noise but is not to be reckoned a force. The Congress party, although it was at a discount insafaras its coming back to power with a large majority was concerned, was the only party with the prospect of forming the government and in that event Rajiv would be its choice. That he would be Prime Minister, did not require the astrologers to tell us.

The Weekly knew it too, but surely it would be a sho't in the arm for it with the circulation of the weekly fast declining and many of its prospective readers addicted to astrology. The number of the Weekly came out even while the body or the remains of Rajiv Gandhi were being put together for cremation. Rajiv was to address a Congress party rally at Sriperambudur, near the Tamil Nadu capital of Chennai, and was introduced to his assassin-to-be by the Congress party candidate on whose behalf he was to address the rally. The astrologers knew pretty little of the lurking fear that the LTTE of Sri Lanka could be a menace for the alleged or real wrongs which Rajiv, during his earlier regime as Prime Minister, could have inflicted on its leader,

V. Prabhakaran, and threat was the bonehomie between the Tamils of India and of Sri Lanka as the Congress party was at that time supporting the LTTE in the island.

The astrologers knew nothing of the kind and, in fact, knew of no danger to Rajiv's life. They made no mention of any danger to Rajiv's life in their forecasts. That the astrologers were made to look fools goes without saying and the Weekly lost its remaining credibility but its editor at that time rose in the estimates of the Shiv Sena supremo to manage a Rajya Sabha seat for himself. He is known to be good friend of the bollywood crowd also. The mention of the Weekly's number is, however, relevant in the context of the men's double role on the UGC's action on astrology. On the one hand, they jolly well publish all manner of forecasts and yet, on the other hand, criticise the UGC and Joshi for introducing the astrology course. It is curious that the CPIM Chief Minister of West Bengal, Buddhadeb Bhattacharyee, convened a conference of fellow sympathisers of his among the Chief Ministers. But the Madhya Pradesh Chief Minister and an important Congress leader, Digvijay Singh came out within four days of the CPIM conference fully endorsing the UGC's decision. He is not only an important leader of the Congress party but a wise man in his own rights who came back to power in the face of the forecast to the contrary in the form of an election survey. Budhadeb's effort seems to have gone in vain.

The UGC's decision on astrology is debatable in the extreme. Whether a high-powered body should have entered the arena at all when the scientific nature of the so-called science of astrology is far from proved. The media cater to the human frailty and know that their circulation would fall the moment they discontinue the weekly forecasts. The point of to make is that while the approach is all right as the publication of the forecasts is concerned they, the print media and some TV media which carry programmes on astrology, cannot at the same time criticise the UGC and Joshi.

There is no dearth of men and women who would want an astrologer to read their horoscope or look at their palm, if you are a politician your curiosity is all the more. The media are, therefore, totally dishonest in opposing the UGC and Joshi's love for astrology while they recklessly publish forecasts and cater to the well recognised human frailty. It is a recognised craving among all human beings to know in advance what is going to happen to them and to that extent Hindu astrology is widely prevalent even among those who do not adhere to their faith just as the Hindus embrace tarrot cards and all the gimmicks of Western astrology.

But we must make it clear that the teaching of courses in universities, particularly the Sanskrit universities or those with a bias in favour of Sanskrit learning, on 'Paurihitya' among the Hindus is right even as the UGC would be totally justified in making the learning of the priestly functions of other religions. The demand for well educated Purohits and Pandits among the Hindus and Hindu communities in the Indian diaspora is growing constantly. It is not a question of Hindutva enjoying preference but the totally unlearned Purohits being weeded out by the availability of the university trained graduates to work as Purohits. The leading paper calls the Hindu ceremony of wedding as "Saptapati". The correct word is "Satpapadi", seven steps which the bride and the bridegroom have to take to solemnise their marriage, before the fire. Does the knowledge available not require a brushing up.

The media approach is suspected to be dishonest. As

an example, the *Hindustan Times* editorial comment in a recent Editorial can be cited. The paper looks askance at the attitude of the two Congress Chief Ministers, already mentioned-Madhya Pradesh CM, Digvijay Singh and the Kerala CM, A.K. Antony, who gave saffron colour the clean chit in their public pronouncements. The paper is believed to be under the thumb of a lady of the Birla clan, Shobhana Bhartia, who is under the illusion that the Congress party must be supported. The paper's editorial comment is not consistent, when it attacks two illustrious Chief Ministers and wise leaders of the Congress party, rebuking them for their support to the BJP when they are showing realism and wisdom.

Bhartia's concern is not only about the Congress retaining its purity but also about the alleged attacks on some Christians in mostly Congress ruled states. Her grandfather may have built temples instead of mosques and churches but she must show respect for the Congress ideology which pretends that Indian secularism is sullied if some Christian places of worship are attacked. The Minorities Commission contains representatives of the Christian Community and Christians round the country may be enjoying the fruits of their labour, which the Constitution protects, but she is not happy if the paper is not attacking what she regards as the BJP ideology. Unfortunately, the editor of the paper is more interested in his TV appearances. She has thus more time on her hands to turn an important paper into a Congress paper and against the NDA. It may be concerned about the scientific temper but the weekly forecasts regularly appears under the name of the author, so that you know what the stars have to tell you about your future.

Notes and References

1. Broadcast Journalism: Basic Principles, S.C. Bhatt, Har-anand Publishers, Delhi-1993.
2. *The Times of India*, Delhi, May 23, 2001, and *Hindu*, Delhi, May 23 and 24.
3. *The Times of India*, Delhi, February, 28, 2000 "Urban India getting more permissive". "Sex is in but awareness is not", the same paper, Feb. 23, 2001.
4. "Kant finds fault with media coverage", *Times of India*, Delhi, February 16, 2000.
5. "Getting the frogs out of the well", guest column by M.S. Aiyar, the *Hindustan Times*, Delhi, September 2, 2001.
6. "Press should implement self censorship" *Hindustan Times*, Delhi, January 28, 2001 "Times of India" of the same date.
7. *Indian Express*, Delhi, October 26, 2000.
8. The Times of India, Delhi, June 22, 2001.
9. "Unfair to UPSC" is the title of the letter published in the *Times of India*, Delhi, on July 31, 2001, from an Under Secretary of the Union Public Service Commission, in which the official denied a report in the paper that the UPSC had not been fair to the visually impaired candidates. The letter, a long one, was carried without the customary "Our correspondent replies", which amounted to an admission of guilt by the paper which had based its story on a single candidates version.

   The Indian Express, on April 17, 2000, carried a refutation "Not True", a refutation by Homi C.H. Bhabha, that his late father was not made a minister in Nehru's first cabinet under the wrong assumption that he was the noted scientist, Homi Bhabha. This was a fairy tale, current among the tribe of Correspondents, but not true. Obviously, these refutations lend credence to the belief that everything that a newspaper publishes is not the truth.
10. *Indian Express*, Delhi, March 26, 2001.
11. *Indian Express*, Delhi, June 20, 2001.
12. *Indian Express*, Delhi, March 12, 2000.
13. *TOI*, Delhi, December 14, 2000.

Two

Attack and Criticism

The media, the print variety, is going all out to make the Sunday papers gloomy. Special stories are written for this purpose, even if they are not scoops or exclusive stories not included in the rivals edition. It seems that the competition on other days reaches its climax on Sunday. Whether there is a Sunday edition or not, (most dailies do not have), but there was a time when the Sundays were an occasion to bring out special editions of the paper and there were special Sunday papers which the readers could savour at leisure on a Sunday when the family went out possibly on a picnic away from the home and its myriad problems. Now there is also competition to serve special stuff, not available on other days, and the same staff brings out the Sunday edition. In fact, some papers call their Sunday edition as a Sundays paper; witness the *Sunday Times* as if there is separate staff for the Sunday paper and there is a separate organisation as in the case of the *London Sunday Times* whose stories are lifted by some Indian papers.

In other words, the dailies try to fill the want of the reader for a special Sunday paper. In effect, however, what one gets is more of the same, more accidents, more bureaucratic bungling, the railways not being safe for travel, more flood forecasts, more road accidents, hospital strikes if the doctors or Karamcharics oblige, otherwise bungling in the purchase and distribution of medicines, and stories of that nature. Looking at some Sunday papers, we get the feeling that we have to recall what we have said before—the generality of the readers getting to read only the headlines and sports pages, ignoring the gloomy forecasts of the papers and conserving the energies for the week ahead and blaming, like the media, the politicians while the media chase them as they always do.

The general impression sought to be conveyed by the media is that they alone are right, except some notable examples, while everything else is going to the dogs. A large section of the readership is gullible and is impressed and possibly believe what the media tell them but the generality go their own way although there is no let-up on the part of the media in their effort to tell the readers that everything other than the media is going to dogs. If the English cricketers want to believe that their captain, an Indian born is a genius, and the former English cricketers who captured the Doordarshan mike in the commentary room, force it into their ears, with the help of some of the media, like the *Times of India,* the readers forget that the English team lost the test series and drew only the one-dayers. Such is the grip of the media. The result is somewhat disastrous for the country and the people themselves.

When the media play up controversies and the sensational as against the truthful, the aim is to increase the circulation in the competitive world. But circulations are bound to go up even otherwise as statistics reveal provided the news media are well brought out and cater to the readers requirements of hard news as palatably told as possible. We have to admit that what is happening generally around the country or in the world outside, in India's neighbourhood or in distant parts, is not that complmentary or pleasing. The news agencies play also their part and play up controversy and the controversial part of the story so as to catch the attention of the deskman. The slant of the story, as told by the news agency, is also on the controversial and the media, the print as well as the electronic depend largely on them. The bigger papers add their own slant and the story, as done by the agency, is already sensational and the highlights of the news and its focus centre around the controversy. Years ago, I recollect, young journalists were kind of overjoyed while a senior journalist almost shed tears. The occasion was the receipt of the news of almost the entire interim cabinet of Burma, now Myanmar, being killed by what would now be called a terrorist attack. U Aung San was extremely popular and was to the country what Gandhiji was to Indians. Burma was at that time on the eve of independence and was crippled. Now Aung San's daughter is waging a relentless stuggle for democrcy in her country, although she is married to a British. Aung San, it goes without saying, was the Prime Minister of the Interim government and was among those killed.

The controversy in the news room of a news paper was as to how to play the news. The senior journalist had lived in Burma and knew of its problems and the importance of Aung San. The deskmen and the reporters wanted the story to be banner headlined while the senior colleagues wanted it played within proportions. Ultimately, the desk's view prevailed but on second thoughts and in the context of what followed in that unhappy country the feeling cannot be avoided that after all the senior colleague was right. Nobody wanted the news to be suppressed and played down in the alternative, but the large interests of the readers should be borne in mind while evaluating the newsfall. What is worth condemning outright is the tendency among the important media, as we have noted, of creating and twisting the news to suit their requirements. The requirements of sensation. This tendency or propensity is noticed in a number of important media, print as well as electronic. They sort of manufacture news to meet their needs to play up sensation at the cost of the truth.

While this was being written the biggest story broke in the form of the September 11, 2001, attack on New York and Washington, D.C., organised by Osama bin Laden and his Al-Qaida organisation of Muslim fundamentalists. The news was indeed devastating and the United States did not go under but launched an attack on Afghanistan which, under Pakistani tuteledge encouraged and harboured Osama bin Laden. The print media had plenty of time on their hands (until 2 a.m. or 12-30 a.m., as the case may be) but the electronic media rose to the occasion by giving us coverage of the main events. In the process the myth that the American CNN gave the news as it happened went out of the window.

The myth had its origin in the US war on Iraq, albeit under UN auspices, in the early nineties. The agency had the advantage of knowing in advance the timing of the US attacks on Iraq from their base in Saudi Arabia. But the agency could not know of the plans of Osama and the planes hijacked by his men and in suicide attacks flown right in the building of World Trade Centre in which more than 250 Indian white collar workers out of the many employed perished. The Indian electronic media did a good job, including the media-despised DD, the national network of Doordarshan which for the same news, sometimes ahead of other channels is not able to garner much of the commercial advertising. *The Times of India* man hired by DD, in expectation of the Samajwadi Party members resigning that day from the UP assembly, that being the expected lead that day, when suddenly, not even to CNN's knowledge, Osama attacked the US.

The US Defence Secretary, as it turned out, was hale and hearty in the Pentagon but Osama directing a plane at the Pentagon raised doubts and the agencies must have contributed to the confusion. After all, sitting here in Delhi, the informed *Aaj Tak* channel as well as the NDTV, operating from the foreign Star channel, could not know the fate of the US Defence Secretary unless the agencies tell them. The worries of translation added to the difficulties of the Hindi *Aaj Tak* who translated the designation of the Defence Secretary Rumsfeld as "Sachiv" instead of "Mantri". In Hindi the term secretary is rendered as sachiv because in India the head of the Bureaucracy is known as Sachiv while the term Mantri is reserved for the political head. In the US, following the UK example, the term for ministers is Secretary, the only case where the US follows the UK which has the distinction of following the US example in all other respects. Fortunately, for the Hindi channel, the confusion cleared up soon and the difficulties of translation were also over.

On the day of the attack, September 11, the print media had an easy time. They have all the time in the world, as we have seen. The print media came out the following day with all manner of headings and without any exception had the banner headlines. *The Times of India* came out on the first day carrying a front page editorial on the attack, being one of the few papers to do so. It tried to shield the Muslim fundamentalists by describing them "so-called". In a couple of days, *the Times* ace correspondent, Siddharth Varadarajan came out with a special write-up in which he berated the US for its "betrayal" of democratic norms while claiming to defend democracy. The same day the paper had an editorial in which it, for a change, supported the government in its approach. Both were contradictory of each other and you could pick youth choice. The paper, however, did a comprehensive coverage of all aspects of the attack, from the Delhi angle as well as the Washington angle. Because Washington was manned by the newly appointed Chidananda Rajghatta (he was earlier *the Indian Express* correspondent in the US capital) and because he was extremely competent and a real newsman the Washington side was well covered.

From Delhi, the paper had more latitude for its pro-Muslim fundamentalist approach and for Siddharth to vent his spleen against the US. It played up the loyalty displayed by large sections of Muslims for Osama through the publication of pictures and favourable news. It went to the extent of dubbing the *Al-Jazeera* channel which highlighted the doings and sayings of Osama and called it the "only source of independent information"[1] and questioned the credibility of the US media by asking "is the American media free"? This is a well known journalistic gimmick, putting the question mark where it is not absolutely certain but it wants the viewpoint to be widely publicised.

The paper was certainly pro-Osama in those days. It had known a tendency to support the cause of the terrorists on several occasions as its pleas for the Muslim fundamentalists clearly show. Fortunately for all concerned the war in Afghanistan, unleashed by the US when the Taliban regime refused to surrender the most wanted Osama and joined its forces with the Northern Alliance, which defeated the force of darkness called the

Taliban, deserted by Musharraf, the military ruler of Pakistan, and the Hamid Karzai led Interim government was installed.

From the highly exaggerated and one-sided accounts of its Kashmir correspondents when the terrorists holed up in a mosque surrender the paper headlines, the siege ends, ignoring the surrender aspect, playing up the terrorist attacks and playing down the security forces success in gunning down the terrorists, special interview with the Lashkar-e-Toiba chief in all these developments the paper displays its fondness for the terrorists and Islamic fundamentalists. Of course, it does it so subtly as not to fall foul of the authorities and hoodwinks its readers all the while. Examples can be cited times without number, of its liking for the so called victims of alleged high-handedness when the fundamentalists are caught with their pants down. It is anxious to prove that it is ever vigilant to protect the honour of the Muslim minority, in fact, the sole protector.

However, the publication by the *Times of India* of a letter by a citizen, Subhash Sood, has to be noted. Said Sood:[2] "The world reacted with shock and disbelief when they saw the gruesome tragedy...." He, of course, referred to the September 11 attack launched by Osama's men. He said there had been a major intelligence failure, but not a single TV channel focussed on the American opposition leaders or people who could have criticised the American administration for its failure. "In fact, from their coverage it seemed that all opposition leaders have been supporting the government completely."

Sood then contrasted the behaviour of the US media and the opposition with the Indians. He said: "Now imagine the same happened in India. Our TV channels would have immediately started criticising the government for its security and intelligence lapses as they did during Kargil. They would have invited countless opposition leaders into news studios for panel discussions. These attention-starved leaders would have run down the government and scored political points....." There are various channels which specialise into one-sided presentation of views, Sood should have added. This letter (it appears the letter was carried because of "Connections") exposes the motives of the media which use, or misuse the freedom enjoyed by the media under the Vajpayee regime, to malign it and its security and intelligence agencies and the opposition leaders and critics who are willing to be tools of propaganda.

The media had achieved its main purpose of choosing sensational presentation of things and events. In February 2000 Prime Minister Vajpayee had uttered[3] a friendly warning not to tamper with facts and said immeasurable damage was done when the Press (he should have said the media) ignored the facts and proceeded on its own assumptions. But obviously it was rather late and highly misplaced as the print media, and even the electronic version, had gone much ahead and made criticism its sole objective. Vajpayee said he was not daunted by the media criticisms but wanted it reserved for the editorial pages. Vajpayee did not refer to the widely held view that the media must criticise every government action no matter the criticism went against the interests of the country at times. The chairman of the Press Council of India, Justice P.N. Savant, a retired judge of the Supreme Court, went to the extent of saying that the main motive of the press was only profit.

The widely prevalent view and practice in the media

is to make criticism of various things the government, the country, its leadership, the politcians, the BCCI (Board of Control for Cricket in India) and other things except the proprietors of the media and themselves from the word go. Vajpayee wanted criticism reserved for the editorial pages of forgot that, as for as the media are corcerned, criticism begins on the front page and ends on the last page. It is spread over the length and breadth of the paper and the electronic media. It is a part of the correspodent's story and a part of the news agency story which is carried by a large number of media. The meanest reporter begins his story with criticism and ends his copy with more critioism. He interprets, enlarges the facts to suit his convenience, distorts whatever he likes and offers his views as though he is a seasoned citizen who has put in many years of service to the nation.

We have the spectacle of Laloo Prasad Yadav being compared to Gandhi and the demolition by the Taliban regime of the ceturies old Buddha statues beigg justified as the Taliban demolishing it them for the world not taking them seriously. Mind you, this criticism is not in the editorial pages where Vajpayee wanted crisioism reserved by the media and where the Taliban will be lambasted for demolishing the statues and perhaps Laloo will also be flayed for ruling by proxy and making a mess of it. Although there is no assurance of that either but one can be reasonably certain. But if Vajpayee is going to read only the edits, as the papers call them, them he is missing a lot from the word go. Vajpayee wanted criticism reserved for the editorial pages. He forgot that, as far as the various media are concerned, criticism begins on the front page and ends on the last page. It is spread over the length and breadth of the paper and the electronic media. It is a part of the correspondents story and a part of the news agency story which is carried by a large number of media. The meanest reporter begins his story with criticism and ends his copy with more criticism. He interprets, and enlarges the facts to suit his convenience, distorts whatever he likes and offers his views as though he is a seasoned citizen who has put in many years of service to the nation.

Even the *Hindu* which is one of the few print media representatives which treats its copy as factually as possible had a correspondent called Muralidhar Reddy who gave even the criticism of the BJP spokesman's daily briefing by the pressmen during the briefing in his story and ridicule the BJP. Now he is the *Hindu* correspondent in Pakistan and in that capacity is careful in the extreme not to offend the Musharraf-regime. The *Hindu* plays up his copy and even the All India Radio books him from time to time, for God knows what reason. He is as docile in Pakistan as he was critical in India. Just note the difference in his behaviour when he is in his own country and when he is under the watchful eyes of the Pakistani press officers. But *the Hindu*, despite this lapse, is meticulous to present both sides of the picture and continues its straight presentation of news.

For the TV channels there is another "difficulty" because they want their news to be as palatable to the viewers as possible so they imagine. They have to present the news as it comes but they have to guide the correspondent on the ground so that they give a sensational twist to their story. For example, when J. Jayalalithaa had her nomination papers rejected from as many as four constituencies (third happened in April 2001) or when the Supreme Court unseated her for wrongly being sworn in by the governor, a retired Supreme

Court judge herself, the anchor asks the correspondent to file something of the reaction, hostile they would like, but the correspondent tells the anchor that they have taken it rather coolly. It is this anxiety on the part of the anchor which gives away the attitude of the TV channel, of the entire electronic media, to the story.

We will have more to say in a separate chapter on the electronic media. To continue about the general media approach, the BJP is part of the NDA and for that purpose it has decided to put in cold storage several of its pet objects like the uniform civil code, although it is one of the Directive Principles of State Policy under the Constitution. It has pledged to solve the Babri mosque issue by either negotiation (between the communities) and according to the decisions of the Supreme Court. Yet the BJP is often taken as the ruling party and Sangh Parivar (the family of the RSS) is often referred to as the evil doer of the worst kind. What is not in the agenda of the NDA is not in the BJP's agenda because the party is part and parcel of the NDA which is the ruling party at the centre.

The NDA government was sworn in on October 13, 1999 and now it has ruled the country for nearly three years or more than half way in its five year tenure after it won a majority in the September-October elections. The media played up petty issues of the Telugu Desam party and the Trinamul Congress of Mamata Banerjee from time to time but when Mamata came back to the NDA in August 2001 after her party's debacle in the West Bengal assembly elections the media swallowed it and raised no objection.

A recurring theme of the media is supposed to be a BJP-Sangh Parivar secret alliance for which there is no basis. Of course, the media are not bound to follow the official line of the parties and they have every right to report the secret alliance if there is one. But if they go on to attack the BJP in season and out of season on the basis of thin evidence it is virtual violation of the ethical code of journalism. Where is media credibility then? The party may say that the temple is not on its agenda but if the media still go on playing up the VHP (Vishwa Hindu Parishad) claim that they would build a temple at Ayodhya after a certain date (March 12, 2002) and the claim that the temple is an election issue although the BJP in Uttar Pradesh has said from the housetops that it is not, it shows bias. At least you have to recall the BJP's official statement every time you say the temple is an election issue.

The BJP is in power in Gujarat state and would remain so till 2003, winter. In October it changed the Chief Minister Keshubhai Patel, because under him the party was seen to be going downhill as the elections to the local bodies showed. There were other indications in that direction too, like the slow pace of the rehabilitation of the earthquake victims. In a peaceful exercise, Narendra Modi, General Secretary of the BJP was sent from Delhi to take over the reins of the Gujarat government from Keshubhai who showed reluctance at the first opportunity but had to bow out when the party bosses put their foot down.

Meanwhile the media, both the print variety and the electronic channels, had a gala time in reporting the development but often proved false. Keshubhai himself proposed Modi's name and Suresh Mehta who raised questions of juniority and seniority quietly was sworn in as a minister under the Modi regime. The *Times of India*, after much play of names of constituencies ultimately pronounced Kutiyana as the chosen constituency but, despite the *Times* having an Ahmedabad edition, it went wrong because Modi chose Rajkot.

What the future holds for the country is difficult to predict but it is certain that the media has embarked on a course which could lead to dangerous consequences. The media which as Justice Savant pointed out are actuated by profit motive have to ask themselves where they are headed at the rate they are proceeding and glorifying themselves while deprecating almost everything else. They should recognise the fact that the Vajpayee government has the TINA (there is no alternative) factor in its favour, although it has moved several miles in front. Despite the opposition parties and the media almost constantly working against it, the Vajpayee government is not concerned much and goes its way in solving the nation's problems. What is happening now is that depending on a solitary case and without saying so, the media generalise and sometimes they have got to publish a refutation of its own story. The media are out to prove that but for them the country could be worse off.

The ESPN is a sports channel which is viewed frequently in India as it covers live many a cricket match abroad in which many listeners and viewers are interested. Cricket is a game that Indians are interested in or a vast majority of them, and ESPN has almost become Indian, as has the Star Sports, with which it has entered into a collaboration. The Star channels are controlled by a foreigner, Rupert Murdoch, Australian turned American and the government, which remains wedded to the 1955 Nehru decision of not allowing any foreign entry to the media, despite some sympathy for it within the government. But the government allows foreign exchange to be transmitted outside the country by the TV channels.

Sunil Gavaskar, a cricket legend, said on the ESPN once that the Indian media which boasted that in India many things are lagging behind others. He asked: "Where are the Indian media then? Aren't they 25 years behind others?" This was in retaliation when somebody said in the media that Indian cricket was 25 years behind Australian cricket. (Gavaskar is pronounced by many as Gaavaskar, although it is Gaavaskar).

There was no answer to his query. The list of these who point out the many flaws of the media could be long, apart from those VVIPs whom we have quoted, in particular Prime Minister Vajpayee and Vice President Krishan Kant. Among them, are Indian captain Saurav Ganguly and another cricket legend, Kapil Dev; there are many leading observers of the current affairs scene. Farooq Abdullah, Jammu and Kashmir Chief Minister, criticised the electronic media for giving sympathetic coverage to the relatives of the hijacked passengers of IC-814 by the Pakistani terrorists. That was a highly painful experience and the whole atmosphere at the time was surcharged. Crowds of relatives used to roam the streets of the capital entering at will the press conference of the External Affairs Minister Jaswant Singh and others.

The media had a hale of time playing up the relatives who represented whom, one may well ask. They could not do much by way of exclusive coverage so they found the relatives like a godsent news item. The Vajpayee government was engaged in delicate negotiations with the hijacker's representatives and possibly the Pakistan and the Taliban regime of Afghanistan and could not do anything to interfere with the relatives of the hijack victims. In retrospect many things could have been done by the authorities but what is the point of pointing it out now. No government, be it of the Congress party led by the Italian born wife of Rajiv Gandhi, or the People's Front of Surjeet and Jyoti Basu or V.P. Singh could have done much else. Vajpayee should ask Sonia

Gandhi or the Left what could they have done before they criticise this government. "These people (the electronic media) made a gross mistake by projecting the demonstrations and the barging of the people into the Foreign Minister's press conference", Abdullah said.

As stated, the exclusive story would call for a herculean efforts. It was easy for the media to play up the relatives of the hijack victims. Obviously the government was engaged in negotiations how to solve the tangle and could not think of how to settle the relatives ire, but the opposition parties and the media had a unique gift. Nobody thinks of the damage to Indian polity and the short-sighted media think of themselves when they should be thinking of the larger issues involved. They committed the error of treating the demonstration as big news when it was an expression of ire on behalf of the relatives on the hijacked plane.

The media are free and the people watch them or read and study them at leisure but the big publicity the relatives received when the demonstration should have received short shrift remained permanently with the Indian people. For the electronic TV channels whatever is photogenic is news. They hardly ponder whether it is news at all. They in effect project what is essentially non-news, if you think now after the event. Years ago we had the same problem in DD. It had news but no visuals and the producers covered events which had no news value. They told the editors to use the visuals even if they were useless. Now the TV channels have all the freedom in the world so they find it useful to cover the event with camera and play it up in the newscast.

Simply because you have the camera, that is hardly any reason for the TV channels to project non-news as news. You cannot cover anything and everything because the print media does it. Many of these demonstrations are organised, as generally every demonstration is, and more often such shows are put up for the benefit of the TV channels. In other words, they are not only staged but stage managed. Even if they are genuine—and it takes a trained newsman no time to separate the chaff from the wheat—you can cover it maintaining a proportion. The private TV channels have under the Vajpayee dispensation, all the freedom in the world but that freedom has to be used with due care.

As the minorities, mainly the Muslims, are vote bank for the political parties, the electronic media particularly use them for the purpose of making news out of nothing. This is amply proved in the case of the so-called Shahi Imam of the Delhi's Jama Masjid, Syed Ahmed Bukhari. He is ever ready to say nasty things about the United States or about his own government as the media wants. There was a violent anti-US wave of demonstration among large sections of Muslims about the terrorist Osama bin Laden. It died its own death after the US and Northern Alliance victory in Afghanistan and the fact of the flight of the terrorist Osama. But while it lasted it made news and for certain media, like the *Times of India* in the print world, it was a constant theme for photographic coverage.

Bukhari is too hungry for cheap publicity and added to his natural instinct, if there is what is called a cause, he is ready to fly at a tangent. He was ready to say that the United State was against the Muslims, which is sparingly used, but his saying it was un-Islamic was often among his charges. The media would tell you on other occasions of his little or no influence among the Muslim masses but use him nevertheless as the spokesman of the Muslims when it suited their purpose.

Making news at any cost seems to be the purpose of

the TV channels. Some channels are more careful like the *Aaj Tak* which are rewarded and even showered with commercials as the *Aaj Tak* is making one wonder if this channel is a channel of ads with the news just thrown in between. Apparently many people watch it and many ads appearing in the channel one can hardly see elsewhere. Even *Aaj Tak* is not totally immune from the tendency to play up the sensational but many watch its programme with the intention of avoiding to buy the daily paper. Whether the daily newspaper is dispensable if you watch your TV channel for the news in the evening ahead.

In making sensation rather then follow the truth the TV channels, the electronic media, are at a distinct advantage over the print media. The print media are a medium of record and storage because they are used by researchers and others at leisure. Nobody of note has analysed the coverage of a TV channel over many days to find out how a particular event was covered. The TV channels themselves produce an amalgam of their coverage but that is neither here nor there.

To sum up: Both the print media, that is our daily newspapers and the electronic media, the TV channels, play up the sensational rather than the truth which is difficult to project. Whether it is easier or more-audience attracting and therefore more advantageous than going over the narrow and straight path, the media prefer the easy way out as it is reckoned, beneficial because it attracts more readers or viewers and therefore more revenue. But the example of *Aaj Tak* should open the eyes of the media to the ultimate truth. Even while playing in proportion the news as seen by its editors, it attracts a large ad revenue, should give a clear message to the other media.

With the observation that the media generally prefer

the sensational to the straight presentation of the news, we have to add all that we have said before about the two media. The print media are now more sophisticated, more news is now presented in the form of features and more care is exercised in writing news than ever before, more stories being known by their headings, colour being added as an essential element, the Sunday editions of the newspapers being the carriers of sensational stories and the daily editions being the vehicles of peculiar stories, the technological revolution that has come about in the print media of which colour is an important part, the attempt to make the stories more readable but the attempt resulting in making them more complicated are some of the elements noted in the print media.

So far as the electronic media are concerned, they are at an advantage in that have the entire world of the satellite TV technology. They know they are in competition, as are the daily papers, but the electronic media are more conscious. The *Aaj Tak* was an appendage of the Metro channel of DD for a long time and the desire to expand led to its separation, although it does not like to recall. (DD now has yet another TV news, which specialises in rape.) The NDTV, main rival if it can be so called, is yet linked to Star, which is a foreign channel, if the print media in general do not like to remember it, and trying to get separated.

Musharraf was variously painted by the media at the Agra summit. Yet, the *Times of India*, which is full of praise for the Pakistani dictator, wrote in its first editorial "General's tightrope" that "Parvez Musharraf has never had it so bad."[4]

Later, it praised the general which only proved that habits die hard. The paper swayed between K. Subrahmanyam's frank and well analysed comments and others fulsome praise, to which it added its own weight in its editorials, after the September 11, 2001's cataclysmic events. The people perished, included 250 Indian white-collar workers, in the attack on World Trade Centre building alone, much property was destroyed in the attack and other Osama attacks, and it led to a war. Pakistan made a virtual U-turn in its foreign policy as well as internal policy without Musharraf carrying out the promised reforms.

George Fernandes' return to the government provided an opportunity to the media as well as the opposition parties to attack the Vajpayee government and display its venom and lack of responsibility while going in for more juicy stories. Vajpayee's statement that there are no charges against Fernandes meant that the government could not wait endlessly for the Venkataswami Commission to make up its mind. His statement was not reported in full although the media were critical as usual. The resignation of Miss Mamata Banerjee in March 2001 and her subsequent return to the NDA in the August of the same year when she rejoined the governing group has been dealt with earlier. That was connected with the resignation of George Fernandes.

The resignation of George Fernandes as Defence Minister was connected with the Tehelka disclosures. The Tehelka team of clandestine reporters had not been able to meet Fernandes despite their efforts. How could then his resignation be linked with the disclosures? But when the issue came up in the form of a moral problem Mamata raised a question of morality and the atmosphere was surcharged. The resignation was the minimum price that Fernandes had to pay for the crimes of others. But August was a different proposition from March. A retired Supreme Court judge had been appointed for a period of three months and he himself had considered the period sufficient at that time.

How long the Prime Minister had to wait for the commission to report and for it to exonerate Fernandes? Vajpayee saw no time frame of any kind and even now the commission has not reported nor it has issued any notice to Fernandes. All this the media could have recited and if they had done so they would be justified in reporting the opposition leaders' speeches in Parliament. Without saying a word on Vajpayee's action in reinducting Fernandes the media went on reporting from day to day the opposition leader's speeches which was an act of folly.

Besides, they never questioned the action of the Congress party, the left and several others in disrupting the proceedings of the two houses of Parliament without ever questioning the propriety of their action. The same argument would apply here as in the case of other disruption on which we quoted Mani Shankar Aiyar earlier. The Defence Minister had to resign in the circumstances prevailing in March 2001 and there was no use asking Vajpayee that question, as had been done by a journalist of the electronic media. After all, it is the privilege of the Prime Minister to appoint anyone he chooses as minister. There were enough grounds to do so in the case of Fernandes.

What is the position of All India Radio in the game which media play? It is a monopoly medium as long as no questions are raised about the monopoly. The highest court in the country has said that broadcasting is the public domain and the waves which are carried from Broadcasting House belong to the people but AIR is still governed by 4th Charter laid down in the wing of the Shastri Bhavan which houses the I and B (Information and Broadcasting) ministry. Unofficially or otherwise some new bulletins are put out by the FM private media which are mushrooming in the country as AIR recognises the value of the FM auctioning.

Still, AIR bulletins run supreme and nobody has taken a count of the elaborate network that AIR is. It is time somebody in the Finance Ministry took cognisance of the elaborate pool work that AIR does and the Indian language bulletins it puts out from Delhi to be relayed by the appropriate regional stations of AIR. Some time ago, a proposal was mooted that the Indian language bulletins be handed over to the RNUs (regional news units), unhappily placed under the stations which treat the RNUs as stepmotherly children and worse still as unwanted units. That does not absolve the headquarters of its responsibility with its elaborate network of Indian language units which is treats rather badly and the pool which operates round the clock.

Until Nehru's death, AIR had a rather easy time when its responsibility was serious and it was its own monitor. After he disappeared from the scene interference by the PMO and the I and B ministry was a daily affair and except brief periods they used to sit like hawks on the DNS (Director of News Services.....Now the post has been elevated to DG, Director General News), seeking to tell what to broadcast ort what no and tell him how to.

But during the period there were editors and there were DNSs who cared for the credibility of the medium and spent precious time and even risked their job in the process of safeguarding the freedom of their media. There were hard times like the internal emergency imposed by Prime Minister Indira Gandhi. Harrowing times were experienced during the time when in additions to the rigours of the emergency we were to undergo the crippling restrains during the elevations of March 1977. Only those who experienced the rigorous orders from above could know what it was like and our credibility was at stake as well.

Somehow we pulled through this period. There was a full after the storm and while the media freedom was in the air there was no real freedom for AIR.

Then came the Prasar Bharati and a real dichotomy was in place and government servants were made to work as spokesmen of the regime that was nowhere in sight. Only the editors and others working in that capacity are virtually exercising the powers of criticism and looking at the policies of the government as critically as possible. There were old hands in AIR who while drawing their salaries cared for the credibility of the medium, but now there are people in AIR who are expected to even criticise the government and still draw their salary from the government. Unusual dichotomy this under which nobody knows who is supreme. Some people take the freedom too seriously and often indulge in behaviours which are neither here nor there.

All the while they are subject to the whims and caprice of a few people in the I and B Ministry who can transfer them and make them full fledged government servants overnight. This has happened in a few cases already. The result is that while at the Prasar Bharati they behave as though they care only for their freedom they have lot to behave in their new capacity as typical government servants. In their earlier tenure they imitated the worst print media but in their new *avatar* they must conform to the rigours of their new regime.

Until either they return to the old regimentation or exercise with due care, their freedom in the Prasar Bharati media, which absorbs them completely and is answerable to their requirements, this dichotomy will persist which is not good for them or for the organisation. Meanwhile the monopoly of AIR persists and until the audio media is thrown open to the public this situation will prevail. Nobody in the political parties has even the vaguest idea of how the medias freedom is to be preserved. Until the Japanese model or the Canadian example is followed this double situation will prevail. The model is that NHK will function as the national channel while there are many private radio and TV channels in the country. On the same lines, DD and AIR have to function as the national channels and the print media and the electronic media function independently of them.

Notes and References

1. *The Times of India*, Delhi, October 19, 2001.
2. *The Times of India*, Delhi, September 18, 2001, under the heading "Gruesome Tragedy".
3. *The Hindustan Times*, Delhi, "PM: to Press: 'Don't tamper with facts" February 12, 2000, so far as Vajpayee's remarks are concerned.
4. *The Times of India*, Delhi, October 10, 2001.

Three

Goof-ups Galore

The print media are often held up before the young ones as examples of spotlessly clean English, almost as exponents of Queen's English. In the United States you would often be asked: where did you learn such "fine" English form ? The Americans generally think that they alone know the English language. During the fairly long time in that country years ago I was often asked that question. I alternately blushed and got irritated. Here we were religiously pursuing our studies of English but many in the US wondered how we could master the language while not being in that country. At last I was relieved to find that the same question was asked of a native of England, that too of an English teacher. She was spending some time in the United States and the people were anxious to know how she had learnt and mastered the English language.

It would be a gross miscalculation to think that the English print media are excellent vehicles of the English language to impress the aspiring young men and women. Just look at the obituary advertisements in several of our dailies. You would come across, with some honourable exceptions, announcements like "with profound sorrow we inform the sad and untimely demise of our beloved Lala Amarnath.....". Neither the advertisers nor the dailies know that "inform" is not an intransitive verb. It is a transitive verb and must be followed by the person or group informed.

Some advertisers take the trouble of adding after inform "you" or some such word/s. They know the English grammar, more than can be said for those who write the English language day in and day out.

The advertising section of the leading dailies can be forgiven for not knowing the correct form but what about the many writers and reporters of the dailies? You can often come across a sentence like "the Minister of Food informed that India's food production had crossed the 200 million tonne mark". The writers and reporters think that like "say" or "state" inform is also an intransitive verb. Some people mistakenly use "tell" as an intransitive verb when they should specify who was told. The saddest part is that those who should know better do not correct this mistake and it is allowed to go into print.

This is not all. The mistakes are galore. The heading may say one thing while the story another, proper nouns begin often in small letters, a story is sometimes printed after the event and wrong headings are given. 'TDP ministers feel neglected by Centre' was a heading in the leading daily the *Times of India*. The Telugu Desam Party has not joined the central government, although it is part of the NDA (National Democratic Alliance) and supports the government of Prime Minister Vajpayee[1]. Even today, despite the open invitation of the Prime Minister, the party has not joined the Central government, so where is the question of being neglected ? As to the argument that one error can be forgiven, the less said the better. To nullify the argument, it headlined; "Peace mission to check Pak-abetted terrorism", and the story that followed said "Sixty motor cycle riders will proceed to Pakistan....... on January 30". The story was published three days after the event[2].

The goof-up on Republic day, 2002 takes the cake. On

that day the Mumbai edition of the paper, which once upon a time was the flagship of the paper, carried on February 5 a story about the Nightingale of India, Lata Mangeshkar. She fittingly "deserved the Padmavibhushan". In fact, Lata Mangeshkar was awarded the Bharat Ratna in the Republic Day awards announced on January 26, 2001. The fault was discovered by Sucheta Dalal, a former reporter of the paper who now does duty at the *Indian Express*. Apparently, she reads carefully her old paper, a case of nostalgia[3].

Like the contemporaries in the capital and the rest of India, The *Hindustan Times* had once upon a time two editors. One of them was apparently in sympathy with the proprietor's daughter, Shobhana Bhartia, who has featured earlier also. He was Bharat Bhushan, who served once the rival paper, The *Times* in a senior capacity. Before he was sacked, he wrote a column "After Vajpayee Who"[4]. He referred to what he called "the current rumour". He said: "It is difficult to understand the current rumour mongering about his (Vajpayee's) health and memory lapses If his health is fine, then the rumours are strikingly reminiscent of the disinformation tactics associated with the Sangh Parivar. Give the dog a bad name and hang it, Bharat Bhushan followed the adage, he thought he would curry favour with Bhartia, his boss, by referring to the Sangh Parivar.

Actually, Bhushan was not favourably inclined to the Vajpayee regime and his knife was always on Vajpayee. He was apparently sacked a year later. If he thought that Vajpayee's health problem and his so-called memory lapses were mere rumours then a column written by the executive editor of the *Hindustan Times* had no business to refer to rumours, whether circulated by the Sangh Parivar or somebody else. He ran the risk of allowing the *Hindustan Times* to be dubbed a sheet of rumours. Before the executive editor entered the portals of the paper, it was known as a staid paper and his efforts and of a lot of others had the credit of making it lively. In the process, it imitates the rival, the *Times of India*, in more than one respect. It is now more than two years since this was published in a leading daily of the capital and Vajpayee has no major health problem.

It seems there is a competition between the two leading papers in making mistakes. *The Times* which specialises in Hindi headings, unusual for an English daily, has the misconception that its editors know Sanskrit which lends it to commit many mistakes. Once it wrote an editorial[5] "The Secular Mother" in which it referred to Ravana's son and called him Meghanath. The correct name is Meghanada, one who has a voice like the cloud. Then the paper referred to the practice among Indians to treat guests as gods and made a bloomer by combining the two words— "Atithidevo". Then it carried a diary item on Ajit Panja, then Minister of State for External Affairs, and committed a howler "Vasudeva Kutumbakam" often mistakenly called so, for the correct vision is "Vasudhaiva Kutumbakam", treating the whole world (Vasudha) as a family. To refer to it as[6, 7] "Vasudeva Kutumbakam" makes it refer to Krishna who was also known as "Vaasudeva" the son of Vasudeva who was imprisoned by his brother-in-law Kansa in Mathura. The error committed by many is not an excuse for the *Times* to make one more error.

The goof-ups are galore in the *Times of India.* On November 16, 1999, it published, story of Vajpayee's visit to Peterm-aritzburg in South Africa to pay homage to Mahatma Gandhi who was thrown out of the compartment because he was not a European while he was a practising lawyer (Gandhiji was in South Africa as a barrister-at-law) in 1893. The paper printed the date as 1873 when he was four years old, being born in 1869. In the good old days, the editors sat with a blue pencil to point out the mistakes made by the deskmen and proofreaders and they got a copy of the paper the next day as they came to duty. Today's editors are busy with the cocktail parties.

The spelling of Atal Bihari Vajpayee's name is a case in point when spelling mistakes repeatedly committed by the print media are referred to. His name is spelt as BIHARI (the second element) but as given in most English papers it is spelt as BEHARI, thus corrupting the name. The correct spelling is given in many full page and half page ads released by the ministries these days and most of the media publish them but who cares for the correct spelling?

The spelling mistakes should be dubbed as deliberate because there are many occasions to correct it but the media commit the same mistake. The *Indian Express* called the Delhi government's bid for the Asiad 2006 as "last-minute" but the story says the last date for the bid was January 28 while the story was published on the 11th.[8] The paper wanted to highlight that it was a last-minute decision. This should be put down as a deliberate mistake, hoping that the readers would not notice it. Whether the *Hindustan Times* of the same date intended it or not, it described the new foreign secretary as the new foreign minister, "Imamul Haq is Pak's new Foreign Minister" ran the heading.

On the same day, by a coincidence, the *Times of India* committed an error when its long time London correspondent, L.K. Sharma, referred to the then British Home Secretary, Jack Straw as Foreign Secretary. The deskman dared not correct Sharma's mistake even though it was obvious. Sharma was subsequently replaced by another correspondent and in the new British government Straw became Foreign Secretary. That does not absolve the paper although it replaced Sharma not on account of the correspondent committing an obvious error.

On November 15,1999 the paper headlined a Ravi Shastri column "Decision to bat first surprising" when it was the other way about, that is after wining the toss the Indian captain, then Sachin Tendulkar, chose to field. On April 14, 2000, the paper carried a middle headlined, "Congress Well" in which the writer, T.A.E.D' Souza, claimed that Bal Gangadhar Tilak addressed a meeting in Belguam (now in Karnataka) in the 30's. Actually Lokamanya died on August 1, 1920 and the Middle writer took the *Times of India* for a ride, including its readers. Exaggeration and use of the hyperbole and even wrong speculation usually mark the passages of the newspapers which want to scare the readers. The stories from Parliament fall into this category and the readers should take them with a proverbial pinch of salt.

The Asian Age, which specialises in hyperbole, carried a despatch by its correspondent, Seema Mustafa, "NDA is a marriage on the rocks". Whatever it may mean, there is no doubt that it forecast the fall of the NDA. This story appeared on February 5, 2000 and more than two years have passed without the NDA going under. Some of the parliamentary stories are headlined "Lok Sabha rocked" when, as we saw, only a walkout is staged. After the walkout, the MPs routinely attend the session after returning to the house. Some of them participate in the proceedings also. On March 16, 2000 the *Indian Express* published "Apology" in bold letters when it sought to placate the Congress leader and former minister C.K. Jaffer Sharief, alleging a relationship between Reshma Sharief and him. The apology was complete and the paper regretted its error. Jaffar Sharief obliged by withdrawing a suit filed by him against a former executive editor of the paper, Prabhu Chawla, now with India Today.

The stories about Deepa Mehta, film maker, had the *Times of India* in trouble when many readers attacked the paper for giving unwanted coverage to her. R.P. Roy compared her to the notorious Miss Mayo whose book *Mother India* was described by Gandhiji as "drain inspector's report[9]".

The *Indian Express* specialises in publishing denials, although this is quite a frequent occurrence with other papers too. On April 10, 2000 the paper carried a denial of the Chairman of the Airport Authority of India, D.V. Gupta. The story was a diary item in which Gupta was alleged to have called on K.S. Sudershan and discussed with him the privatisation of the airports. In the refutation, Gupta denied ever having met the RSS chief. How the story was published in the first place is a mystery. The *Hindustan Times*[10] denied its own story that the present army chief Gen. Padmanabhan, who was chief of the Southern army command and mentioned as the future army chief as having undergone a bypass surgery. Obviously the story must have been inspired by a rival of the present army chief.

The print media goofed up, and this time they were joined by the electronic media, in reporting Bill Clinton who visited India for a few days in March 2000, a year before he was to step down. This was a case of Jaipur in India (Rajasthan) being mixed up with Joypura in Bangladesh. Many a paper, the *Indian Express* in particular, mixed up the two and caused a near panic in Jaipur. The story was that Clinton arrived in Delhi on March 19 and the next day was Holi, the festival of colour, marking the advent of spring and the day which marks the end of the long winter in north India and parts of east and west India as well. In Delhi, people go mad splashing coloured water and powder on each other and nothing else gets done, not before the day is out.

So, Clinton made off for Bangladesh the next day and it was announced by his security men that he would not visit Joypura, a village of Bangladesh and confine himself to making the most of his Dhaka visit. This was mistaken by the media as if Clinton was cancelling a visit to Jaipur. On March 20, the Holi day, the capital's papers came out with the announcement that his Jaipur visit was off. There was virtual consternation in Rajasthan. The next day, the *Hindu* which is the only Delhi paper to come out because possibly the South Indians do not observe the colour aspect of Holi, being a Chennai paper, said, under the heating "everything in a name" which hardly enlighten you, that Clinton had been advised by his security men to cancel a visit to Joypura which was mistaken for Jaipur by the Indian media, including the Star TV's NDTV, which specialises in scary headlines.

On March 21, the *Hindu* announced proudly that there was no change in Clinton's itinerary and the next day, the *India Express* apologised to its readers about the goof-up. This a tradition that the paper keeps up despite its habit of being in a hurry to announce various things which lands it in a soup as in the present case. The paper has a tendency to give sentence long headings which also is tricky business. On November 9, 1999 the paper's headline, one of the several, ran like this: "Cyber cafe' big brothers' track people's Net moves, hack into accounts" if you can make head or tail of it.

If there is nothing to comment about, there is at least the Sangh Parivar, as the *Tribune's* P. Raman, at the time the paper's Political correspondent found out on November 9, 1999. He linked it to the dual membership issue raised during the Janata Party ruling Madhu Limaye. This is believed to have split the party and paved the way for the return of Indira Gandhi. Hoping that his discussion and recall of what Limaye did to the Janata Party could happen to the Vajpayee coalition in 1999 Raman wrote his column. Alas, the coalition lasted for more than two years after the writing and is slated to last longer. Only if wishes were horses.

The falling standards of journalism and the journalist emerging as a power broker was the lament of an award winner on April 4, 2000. Television journalist, Barkha Dutt, who was chosen for the award in her acceptance speech, said that "the emergence of the journalist as the ultimate power broker, the Rajya Sabha aspirant and the one who throws the best parties and makes to the insides of the cheaply produced supplements, produced by fellow journalists." The journalist was in a self-confessing mood and could speak of the fellow journalists who aspire to Rajya Sabha membership and sometimes get it with an effort but she should more closely look into the NDTV aligned to the Star foreign network, where she is employed.

The Hindustan Times had the following story on December 18, 1999 from Parliament, "The Leader of the House also informed that the government had received additional information and some papers from the Luxemburg pertaining to the (Bofors) case". First of all, it shows that "informs" is widely used by even senior journalists (those who cover Parliament are senior people) as an intransitive verb which is wrong. Luxemburg is a proper noun, the name of a country, and does not take any article. That a grammatically wrong story should be written by a senior correspondent and published by a front-ranking paper of the capital is a bad example of the rules that major dailies follow.

Satyendra Singh, a retired senior officer of the Indian

navy, wrote to the *Indian Express* on January 10, 2000 that the Star TV's appendage, NDTV, had on December 25, soon after the Pakistani hijackers had hijacked the Indian Airlines plane on its IC-814 flight, said in its forenoon bulletin that the hijackers could be Sikhs. This was not the version published by any newspaper or any TV station. Apart from this, the NDTV had erred in reporting that Sikhs and not Pakistan was responsible for the hijacking. Satyendra Singh's main contention was that a whole community, the Sikhs, had been identified with the ghastly crime. That was against the Press Council guidelines... Foreign media also had the distinction, but in India the NDTV has the single honour of carrying the report. Incidentally the *Washington Times* apologised to the Sikh Community for carrying this misleading information but nothing was heard from the NDTV. Satyendra Singh took up the matter with NDTV but there was no response.

The leading paper of India, *The Times of India*, carried on December 10, 1999 a feature "Indians of the Century" in which the martyr Bhagat Singh rightly featured. The paper, however, committed the error of linking his throwing a bomb in the Central Assembly in which none was seriously hurt to his hanging in the Lahore jail by the British. Bhagat Singh was hanged for shooting a British police officer who ordered a baton charge on Lala Lajpat Rai when he took out a procession in the city of Lahore against the Simon Commission, not for throwing a bomb in the Central Assembly as the paper said.

Nine days later, the paper spelt Jawaharlal Nehru as Jawahar Lal Nehru, as if his name is written in two parts. This is a common mistake in north India where it is customary to split up the names, but Nehru did not and the leading paper is expected to know it. This is also stated in the start of this chapter where it is emphasised that the younger generation looks upto the leading newspapers to guide them in such matters. That the writer of the column was Nikhat Kazmi, who is a principal writer of the paper, makes it all the more pertinent. The writer is a talented person who has cured herself of a bias for Muslims in the cinema for which she contributes a weekly feature. Almost cured, we should say, because now and then she lapses into it. (She called the struggling Saif Ali Khan as Shammi Kapoor once.)

In this connection we have to notice the fondness of some in the print media for slang and colloquial words. On January 13, 2000, the Delhi edition of the *Times of India* had a front-page heading "none will flunk class X exams". Flunk, according to the Oxford Dictionary, is "verb US colloquial". It also means fail in examination. On the same day, it had another heading "DUTA wants teachers to stop bunking". Again according to the Oxford Dictionary bunk is slang meaning run away. The question arises who benefits apart from the reporter who displays knowledge of slang words. If the students are above average and know the meaning of the term used they are not impressed and the lowly have to refer to the dictionary, if at all. The Delhi University teachers who are habitually skipping the classes they have to teach care two hoots if they get to read the heading.

The print media as well as the electronic channel cried themselves hoarse about the imminence of an epidemic in Orissa following the devastating cyclone of 1999. They went on predicting it in which AIR joined after its newly acquired freedom but fortunately no epidemic occurred. Recently, when Himachal Pradesh had the misfortune of a few deaths owing to what appeared like plague, the media had plenty scary headlines but thanks to the prompt measures taken by the Himachal government there was no epidemic. Typically the *Times*, Delhi, edition on the first day when the outbreak was mentioned tried to give the impression as if the capital was hit, not Himachal, specially a village in the state. It got the correspondent who specialises in health matters busy without giving any indication in the heading that it was Himachal Pradesh which was hit, not the capital of some unwary readers pick up the paper, all the better for the proprietors.

The love for sensation and the fondness and competition among the media for it make dailies and the TV channels say things in such lurid light that if real tiger were to hit the urban areas the people have had it. Whether the proprietors really encourage it or not we have no means of knowing, but the way they have tolerated it so long would show that they have accepted it. They think that the way to higher circulation is through the sensational stories being highlighted and the truth being hidden. The owners of the print media and the TV channels are the same in several cases and the competition ensures that all the people connected with the media travel in the same boat.

The headlines are supposed to indicate what the story expects to tell the reader or viewer and often the heading saves the story but sometimes the headlines are misleading and sometimes they are devoid of meaning. What do you make of a heading like this "Rollover Sinha beg to differ" and "Short on big ideas, Sinha lets government get away"? If you care, the story was about the Budget 2000-2001 presented by the Finance Minister Yashwant Sinha to the Lok Sabha of February 29. The first headline is from the *Times of India*, of March 1, and the second from the *Indian Express*, both from Delhi. They reflect the story-writer's and the headliner's shortcomings. You may well ask the meaning of the term "Rollover Sinha" and its place in the scheme of things except to show the bias of the correspondent. How the term "beg to differ" makes sense and "how is he short? on big ideas" and how Sinha lets his government get away? Specially when he is short of big ideas?

No wonder one of the regular readers of the *Hindustan Times*[11] wrote to the paper and accused the editorial staff of headline hunting. He does not spare even the TV channels and accuses them of the same thing. The writer, Subhash Chandra Agrawal of Delhi charges the media with trying to gain cheap popularity by presenting sensational news stories which sometimes are against national interest.

What the media think of themselves and what some readers think should be at variance with each other if what the reader quoted above is true. In no other situation perhaps this is true than in the stories of the Jammu and Kashmir militants, most of them sponsored, aided and abetted and even coordinated by the Pakistan ISI (the Inter Services Intelligence). Look at *the Hindu* headline on the celebrations of Republic Day 2000. Although the celebrations passed off peacefully some rockets fired by the terrorists pennel in *the Hindu* deskman to headline a three column story as "Rocket attacks mar R-Day in Jammu". This was following some rocket attack with eight rockets in the Jammu area. The security forces gunning down seven terrorists is not good news for the staid paper that *the Hindu* is. Its Srinagar correspondent, by the name of Shujat Bukhari, who somehow spells his name as "Shujaat" gave the details to the paper about the activities of the terrorists as well as the Huriyat Conference which called the customary strike.

Is it necessary to project the activities of the terrorists in such detail? It is widely believed that the Srinagar based correspondents are either in sympathy with the terrorists or afraid of them so that they paint them in acceptable colours and report their activities in full and throw doubts on the integrity of the security forces and they protect themselves thus.

The whole structure of terrorism in Jammu and Kashmir is such that people in India are inclined to trust the media when they project them for what they are worth—as pure and simple terrorists. But the constant projection of them as people who are cruel for a cause and doubting the integrity of the security forces upsets all calculations. What Pakistan wants is full control of Kashmir which it believes the free media of India will help in getting. Papers like *the Hindu* and the *Times of India* are not interested in playing the Pakistani game but unwittingly they do so and their full coverage to the Kashmir problem is an aid to Pakistan and the Indian media are thus playing into the hands of the enemy. If sections of the media honestly believe that India should not retain Jammu and Kashmir they should say so and not hold their readers and viewers to ransom. If the audience still wants to plug for their favourite paper or channel let them be known as subscribers to the media which are openly against the national interests. For papers and TV channels which support the Indian cause, they must ask themselves where they are going. There has to be a balance between national interest and credibility. This kind of coverage for terrorist activity is no good.

Finally, the SMS language, the SMS stands for short message service and if you believe the *Sunday Times*, the so-called Sunday paper of the *Times of India*, or the Sunday edition of the paper falsely called the Sunday Times, there are 20 billion messages sent worldwide in SMS[12]. One need not take at face value the claims on behalf of the SMS. We have media which are so self-centred that they cannot think beyond their noses, we have at least 350 million people who live below the poverty line but also have 250 million who have enough to spend on all necessities of life. What is more, they have even some money to spare for luxuries which includes the monthly cable operators as they bring many satellite channels to enrich their lives, and even spend on their daily newspapers. This number can be even higher. No studies have been made and surveys conducted but the fact remains that India has 250 million people or more in the bracket which includes the "Rich" middle classes. Add to this the upper classes and the really rich and a figure of 300 million people is not unreasonable.

But the substantial number of people who are below the poverty line have also to be taken into account and it is a sobering thought when wider issues are debated. The relevance of the media debate when India has to carry a large number of people who have extremely limited means of living is also to be considered. But we have to live in this semi-modern world in which big ideas have also their place as well as the fate of millions who eke out a living somehow.

Notes and References

1. *The Times of India*, Delhi, July 29, 2000.
2. The Delhi edition of the paper, 2-2-2001.
3. *Indian Express*, Delhi, February 5, 2001.
4. *The Hindustan Times*, February 4, 2000.
5. *The Times of India*, Delhi, October 19, 1999, November 12, 1999.
6. *Ibid.*
7. *Ibid.*
8. *The Indian Express* Delhi, February 11, 2000.
9. *The Times of India*, Delhi, February 3, 2000.
10. *The Hindustan Times*, Delhi, March 7, 2000.
11. *The Hindustan Times*, Delhi, September 23, 2000.
12. *The Times of India*, Delhi, September 2, 2001.

Four

Bias in the Print Media

In the previous chapters we have said on more than one occasion that the media rightly regard the principle of conflict as the basis of news they present. We have also emphasised that the media balance the presentation and take into account the overriding principle of credibility and truthfulness. This principle cannot be sacrificed at any time. Consistent with it, news can be presented in an attractive manner and style. Some media condemn the others in wrongly evaluating, for example, the importance of the Shahi Imam of Delhi, Syed Ahmed Bukhari, who makes extreme statements from time to time. Some of the papers say that he commands little influence on the common Muslims although he leads the prayers on Friday when Muslims congregate in large numbers and he often addresses them in provocative terms.

The bias in the dailies, particularly that section which operates in English and considers themselves above fellow dailies (in Hindi and other Indian languages), comes in the form of always needling the NDA (National Democratic Alliance) which has been ruling the Centre from October 1999, showing some allies of the BJP, the dominant partner, as different and always project the ruling alliance as if it is in a state of flux. The English media are imitated in many ways by the Hindi and other Indian language papers although they may not admit it. So this evil travels to the other papers as well. As we pointed out in dealing with parliamentary hold-ups which is a matter of frequent occurrence now, they project this phenomenon as "rocking", as a calamity rather than an everyday event and this is taken up by the Indian language press as well. Then there are the news agencies, PTI and UNI, which seem to cater to the English papers primarily and follow their language of hostility and ridicule.

Add to this the attitude of the leading paper, the *Times of India*, and to a lesser extent the *Hindustan Times*, which is one of super-adviser on all matters, holding the paper supreme in all respects and in a position to give words of wisdom to the government, political parties, literary men, men of science and technology, all sportsmen and a galaxy of other people. It is the function of the media to report to all and sundry but there a limit and the leading paper almost crosses the limit from day to day. Perhaps the reason why the paper is bought more than the others, apart from the elimination of competitors[1], is this attitude of superiority which the readers like to share as a psychological device. In one respect, the *Hindustan Times* claim to fame is true, the *TOI* has become a Congress paper like the HT, both in a suitable manner.

In projecting Pakistan there is no rival of the *Times of India* as in the matter of Osama bin Laden, now hiding in Pakistan. It is well known that its ace correspondent, Siddharth Varadarajan, justified Taliban destroying the centuries-old statues of the Buddha (what an irony that a man named after the Buddha in his pre-Buddha days should be justifying the demolition) and should visit Pakistan for an interview with the Lashkar-e-Toiba chief before he was symbolically imprisoned by Musharraf.

In a Sunday edition of the paper[2], the editors posed

the question "Why is America afraid of Al-Jazeera?" The channel is no longer heard of any more, the *Times* having forgotten it altogether. The United States has never answered the query but the falseness of the claim made for the channel by the paper was proved wrong on many occasions. Remember the paper once described the channel as the only source of independent news (about Afghanistan). Now there is an interim government in Afghanistan where Simla-educated Hamid Karzai is its leader who visited India in February 2002. The Taliban is finished and almost down and out, Musharraf has made a U-turn in foreign and domestic policy. Despite the *Times of India*, the United States is victorious in the US-Afghan war in 2001-02. Surprisingly no man of the paper was harmed in the war as the paper never sent any of its correspondents to the war theatre. The *Hindustan Times* at least sent its correspondents to Pakistan from where the Musharraf regime had him summarily expelled. Among resident correspondents is the *Hindu's* B. Muralidhar Reddy who faithfully copies the handouts of the Pakistan government and they are proudly published in the paper.

No doubt, the *Times of India* is the leading Indian paper and is one of the best in the world but it assumes superior airs. All great men and institutions have to have some humility which is missing in the paper. In many respects, it often creates a scare and quietly says after some days that the scare should have been ignored. In a front page story it advised the readers to relax in October 2001. "Relax, it could be just talcum powder"[3]. Just before the story was published, the paper had created a virtual fright among the readers over the anthrax story, a creation of the west to which the *TOI* is extremely vulnerable. The world news agencies, of course, created a scare, a new kind of terror, but it is the duty of the newspaper sometimes not to follow the lead of the news agencies.

Of the forecasts the paper made, the less said the better. For example, its sports editor personally predicted on the basis of information with him that the President of the BCCI (Board of Control) for Cricket in India, then A.C. Muthaiah, would be re-elected. The readers believed the forecast as there was an intense tussle between Muthaiah and former ICC (International Cricket Council) President, Jagmohan Dalmiya. Dalmiya was without any major job after his term at the ICC as President was over although he was President of the Bengal Cricket Association. To the surprise of the sports-loving readership of the *TOI*, which is large, it was Dalmiya who was elected and not Muthaiah. As stated before, there was intense tussle between the two and the readers of the paper would not have minded the paper going without the story, instead of a wrong forecast being projected. Possibly the sports editor did not have any axe to grind in protecting one of the candidates but he suffered a fall nevertheless.

Then there is the forecast "Death penalty may be abolished" prominently headlined and credited to Akshaya Mukul, one of the two correspondents the paper took over from its rival in Delhi. He is in conflict with various authorities for his wrong reports but the report, carried on October 18, 2000[4], had some interest. It is now nearly two years since the report appeared but there is no move to abolish the death penalty. In fact, already the Supreme Court has circumscribed the powers of the trial courts, in its judgement on the rares of rare cases in which the death sentence could be awarded. The trial courts prefer to award the other alternative sentence of life imprisonment and be done with the trial. The award of death sentence is long subject to approval by the respective high court even as it is. A quick look at the report would convince anyone that it is highly speculative and that is why there is no move yet after two years when the report first appeared that nothing seems to be moving in the direction of the prediction becoming a reality.

Though the number of forecasts going wrong must be legion, we cannot resist the temptation of citing a report which went wrong. Govinda, the popular actor of the silver screen, was roped in by a foreign TV channel, Sony, and the first *Chappar Phad Ke* item was broadcast. In the first review of the programme the *TOI* forecast that the programme was a great success and it would last and help Govinda's film career also. From thrice a week, the programme came down first to twice a week and then it was once a week only and it finally folded up even before the *Kaun Banega Crorepati* which was its rival did. Whether Govinda expected his film career to be boosted by the programme we were not told by the paper when the programme packed up.

Writing in the *Hindustan Times* of September 23, 2000, Subhash Chandra Agrawal of Delhi took the paper to task for speculating on Vajpayee's health. A reference was made in one of the earlier chapters to Bharat Bhushan the executive editor of the paper openly commenting on Vajpayee's health and pretending to condemn the "rumours" while circulating one more rumour himself. It is now more than two years when the story first saw the light of the day in *HT* columns but Vajpayee has not obliged the paper or many of his "well-wishers" in the media. After heavily criticising the paper, the letter-writer Aggarwal expresses the hope that "in national interest, the media should understand its responsibility to act sensibly.

The Government should also resist itself from giving unwarranted clarifications which tend to highlight disturbing news stories though these may have passed unnoticed by the public."

Although the paper had the good sense to carry the letter it had alongside it a cartoon showing a vehicle (possibly an ambulance) and a red cross sign painted on it with the words 'PM' prominently written on it at the back. The story and the letter appeared in September 2000, nearly two years ago and Vajpayee is still alive. The *HT* has become a Congress paper and it is fun to write about Vajpayee's health. Such is the freedom allowed under his liberal regime. In Pakistan, the editor of *News* had to flee his country after publishing a story which offended the ISI (Inter Services Intelligence). This is a big difference about the media in the two neighbours but there is no end to newsmen seeking similarities between the two. Agrawal, whose letter was published with the heading "Headline Hunters", an appropriate heading, one must say in fairness, compliance: "It is disturbing that the Indian media is working hard to gain cheap popularity....".

The media, specially the print variety, are full of stories and writings which could not be imagined under the Congress regime nor in the British days. The media have full freedom to express themselves and they are utilising it to the hearts' content. It is virtual violation of the rules of the game and a total exploitation of the freedom permitted by the NDA government. There is nobody to tell the media that they are misappropriating somebody else's domain. The opposition is of the view that the time presents the best opportunity to topple the NDA government and the media in the name of the freedom of the press, are going all out to highlight the opposition's attack. The role of the media in the less than satisfactory performance of the BJP in the four states assembly elections early in 2002 is a commentary on the media, hammering the NDA government all the while.

Like TV serials dragging on and on till the channel asks them to go, the print media are attacking the government and the NDA and only the people of India are the ultimate judge of their performance. They display the same tendency over and again and playing up the neighbours and their rulers. For example, the *TOI* was never tired of praising Gen. Pervez Musharraf, military ruler of Pakistan, who usurped power in October 1999 and will continue in power as long as he is willing to rule. This despite many of its readers writing to it warning it to stop doing it. Reader L.D. Bhatia, writing to the paper in July-August 2000, soon after the Agra summit said: "I must be candid enough to say, however, that of all the Indian newspapers that went out of their way to create unnecessary hype and hoopla over the general's visit (to India), the *Times of India* led the way in lionising and glorifying the general."

The bias in the print media is not only manifest in the form of the paper displaying pro-Pakistan inclinations but in its actual coverage and choice of words to describe the hostile attitude of Pakistan and its leaders towards India. If the *TOI* is bent upon showing its pro-Pakistan bias, the *HT* shows much concern for the Christians at home. No doubt, some attacks take place on Christian institutions and individuals but care must be taken specially by the media, which are read or seen by many readers and viewers, to distinguish such attacks from ordinary burglaries and criminal activities—a daily occurrence. Christians are part and parcel of the nation and they enjoy, under the

Constitution, the same rights as other citizens which makes no distinction between believers of one faith and another[5].

By virtue of the progress made by them in education, the Christians enjoy a much higher percentage in the higher and ordinary services of the government as well as in the private sector. There is no discrimination of any kind which would make meaning of the sustained campaign of the *Hindustan Times* with prominent display of the so-called attacks on Christians and their institutions. The *HT* is a long standing paper, in fact the oldest daily of the capital and the purchasers of old newspapers used to shout, not long ago, "Hindustan" (nor to be mistaken for a Hindi daily from the same stable, a daily of some substance) and it was known for its staidness. The paper now has become a Congress daily, as we saw in earlier chapters, and many of its correspondents devotees of the Congress President, Sonia Gandhi. An important correspondent, who also happens to be the bureau chief once predicted a rally of Sonia to be a huge affair and it turned out to be a flop.

Its Ahmedabad correspondent specialises in Christians being attacked. (His favourite, Shanker Singh Vaghela, once the Chief Minister of Gujarat, is no longer heard of). In Indonesia Christians are routinely killed by Muslims (Indonesians are by nature tolerant but this is happening) but in India, despite the attacks prominently displayed by a section of the print media of which the *HT*, Delhi, is a leading paper, no Christian has been killed. It is remarkable that in spite of so called attacks on Christians and Christian institutions not a single Christian has been done to death.

The attacks have been investigated by the Minorities Commission in which its Christian members took a prominent part. The commission came to the conclusion that Christians had been attacked, not as Christians but as individuals. All the correspondents who covered the so-called attacks did not tell us why a proselytiser distributed to the Hindu pupils of a school in Rajkot (Gujarat) if his intention was not to convert them to the Christian faith. The media, a section of them, raise questions of the secular values being attacked in such cases but they seldom find out why the proselytisers are active.

What is happening is that the Hindus are now more aware of the attempts on the part of some Christians and Christian institutions to convert the unwary Hindus and therefore, there is some noise about the so-called attacks. The loud and media-savvy leaders of Christians are partly responsible for this phenomenon. The correspondents may get a story which the papers following the anti-Hindu policy gladly publish, but neither the reporters nor the papers realise the harm done to the cause of Indian secularism. In particular, the foreign correspondents stationed in India, who know no Indian language except English, lift the stories from the *HT* and other papers of its ilk, as they always do. The Indian Press in its English version comes handy to them and provides readymade material which they can lift and play up. As stated often before, the English papers do not mind if an image of India is projected which is not a true image. The Central government appointed a sitting Supreme Court judge to inquire into the attack on the Australian missionary who was killed in Orissa, then a Congress ruled state, and finally the main accused was found and arrested. His trial is in progress. That an Australian missionary was killed in the company of his two sons, both children, is a sad affair but the presence of a missionary raises questions.

The media are justified in portraying events—the so

called attacks on Christians and Christian institutions, the trouble in Gujarat following the killing of 58 Ayodhya returnees, or the Ayodhaya story itself, but they must not fall prey to the edict 'sensation, not truth is our guiding principle. For example, the *Times of India* had not acknowledged to this day that the situation in Ahmedabad has returned to normal, not in its headlines at least. Why fight shy of truth, when it went out of its way to portray the 'killings' in Ahmedabad and elsewhere in Gujarat. Many readers are reading only the headings and not the full story in which the paper noted that a kind of normalcy had returned to the city. When the paper has an Ahmedabad edition and has at its disposal competent staff why it should fight shy of the truth? But the competent reporters are to be employed for another, more sinister, purpose.

The stories are so complicated, by the media themselves, that it is difficult to separate the truth from its more murkier aspect. In the name of less sensation we are not making a plea for keeping out stories of a controversial nature. Far from it. What we are pointing out is the total sensationalising of the events when there is extreme need of less dependence on sensation. For example, the leaders of opposition parties, including Sonia Gandhi, the Congress President, visited Godhra for a few minutes and Ahmedabad for a little longer, they declined to call on the Gujarat Chief Minister, Narendra Modi, whose resignation they were demanding. Did any media point this out and condemn the attitude of the opposition leaders as arrogant and they did not show any courtesy and missed an opportunity of knowing at first hand the reasons why Modi acted in a particular way. The opposition leaders showed thereby that political capital was all that they were interested in as much as the media as usual. We have to caution the readers that when we refer to the media we are concerned that an influential section of them are interested in sensationalising the events.

We are concerned at the developments, at which the media are proceeding because the time may come when an unfortunate development may occur. The *Times of India* has other purposes in mind; specially, the return of the Congress party under the leadership of Sonia Gandhi, which it has made its mission. It attacks the NDA and the BJP relentlessly for that purpose and it subtly supports the Congress. Witness its projection of the fourteen states under the rule of the Congress party on the morrow of election results in four states in February 2002. It employs one of its numerous reporters to keep a watch on Priyanka Gandhi-Vadhra and projects her in season and out of season. The other media, however, to take notice lest they are caught unawares.

Incidentally, the paper made a forecast that the former BJP President, Bangaru Laxman, might be rehabilitated and even taken into the central cabinet. It may be recalled that Bangaru was a Minister of State for Railways when he resigned to take over as President of the BJP. The paper seemed to have based its forecast on the flimsy ground that Bangaru was elected chairman of the Rajya Sabha House committee, because for the Rajya Sabha nominations he was not considered by the BJP for re-election from the state of Gujarat. Instead the person, Jana Krishnamurthy, who succeeded him in the BJP President's post was nominated by the party.

Rajya Sabha nomination is a safe passage, like a mythical ticket to heaven, because the candidate does not have to incur any expenditure to get elected as the Lok Sabha candidates have to incur and once elected he is safe and secure for a six year period. The Rajya Sabha membership is for six years whereas the Lok Sabha members' tenure is for five years and that too if the house is not dissolved earlier by the President. The tenure of the 11th and 12th Lok Sabha was terminated by President Narayanan. The Rajya Sabha membership is often treated as a political luxury by many people, except when the respective party MLAs do not carry out the party high command's order as happened in the case of the Congress party candidate in West Bengal in 2000.

It is risky and even dangerous to depend on the forecasts of the *Times of India*. Why the paper persists in its attitude one does not know. It forecasted Mulayam Singh Yadav as the Prime Minister when Deve Gowda was overthrown by the Congress which was supporting the United Front government at the Centre from outside in 1996 and 1997. During the hectic negotiations for the new Prime Minister, Mulayam was supported by the CPIM leader, Harkrishan Singh Surjeet, and he seemed to be keen that his name come out in the media. Nothing like the *Times* because what the paper says so many believe it to be gospel truth. As it turned out, I.K.Gujral was elected and ruled for a few months as the Prime Minister of India. Gujral had a good rapport with the then Congress President, Sitaram Kesri, who trusted Gujral as a former Congressman of long standing. That was a calculated blunder of the *Times* for which it did not suffer much. The paper persists with the Correspondent concerned in spite of being let down by her. The organisers know that as long as it retains the trust of the readers and advertisers it has nothing to fear!

It is the reason for sending a correspondent from Delhi when Kanpur was affected by riots in which the mischievous elements killed a senior civil official. Kanpur is next door to the State capital, Lucknow, where the paper has competent correspondents, having Lucknow edition. The Students Islamic Movement of India (SIMI) was allegedly responsible for the riots and their leaders were found in the hotel room of the correspondent. The SIMI was not then a banned body and the leaders moved about somewhat stealthily but on the whole freely. Akshaya Mukul, the correspondent, is known to be of the views of Siddharth Varadarajan and is one of the two correspondents imported by the paper from its rival in the capital. As we said, the owners of the paper and the business executives who actually run the organisation care two hoots for the readers views as long as their various business enterprises prosper, including the websites, the Planet M where it encourages young men and women to mix, no matter the paper has to comment later on the permissiveness in our society. So they occasionally publish views contrary to what the paper preaches but carries on as before. Readers should know that most writings of this nature are however consigned to oblivion.

The *Hindu* often carries stories contrary to its views but it highlights and presents in a straightforward manner many stories on the first page and inside pages. It is particularly careful about presentation of different points of view but its editorial policy is against the NDA government. The *Indian Express*, a truly national daily because it has several editions from different cities, except eastern India, has no business policy worth the name. It has Delhi and Mumbai editions but has little or no business from these two major cities and has to depend on classified ads emerging from the Central and state governments, like the *Pioneer*. Its peculiar headline policy, where each double column headline has to be a complete sentence, and its general approach seems to be scaring business class and in the absence of any rival the *Times* prospers and keeps on playing its double role of running with the hare and hunting with the hounds. The *Indian Express* is no less sensational and its regard for the truth is not noticeable but it often carries different points of view, both in its editorial columns and news.

The other newspapers, the Calcutta and Delhi *Statesman* and the *Telegraph* of Calcutta and the various editions of the paper, *Asian Age*, should be mentioned and noticed. The *Asian Age* often strikes one as the paper which has ample space for news but contains the views of a section only. It does not seem to be patronised by the large business sector nor by the government sector in the matter of ads. Except the *Statesman* and the *Telegraph*, to an extent, and the *Hindu* to some extent, the media are in the same category more or less.

There are provincial papers and there are metropolitan papers but as we said, there are news agencies which cater to the requirements of the news media of the English newspapers above all else and compete to a great extent with each other and the world news agencies and behave as though they do not belong to this world. They are mostly conscious of the need to project the point of view of the media.

Reference was made earlier to the Pakistani editor of a prominent paper, the *News*, Shaheen Sehbai who lost his editor's job for not bowing to the dictates of Musharraf's men and defying the midnight call to keep out a story. Now the *Times of India* has partially redeemed itself by publishing an interview with him[6] titled "The Daily Noose", to rhyme with the papers name and an apt heading to describe the plight of journalists under the Pakistani military dictator, the interview is extremely revealing.

In the interview, Sehbai told the paper that on February 16 the *News's* Karachi correspondent, Kamran Khan, (the paper is based in Lahore where its much older Urdu paper, the *Jung* is also located although it has a Karachi edition also). The story quoted Omar Sheikh (the same person who India released for the safety of over 100 passengers in the IC 814 affair in December 1999 and was immediately let loose by the Pakistani ISI) that he was behind the attack on the Indian Parliament on December 13, the Kashmir Assembly attack in October 2001 and other terrorist attacks in India. The story was intercepted by the ISI (how meticulously it listen's to such stories). Shortly after 1 a.m. the editor got a call from the principal information officer of the Pakistan government, Ashfaq Gondal.

Gondal, who once did a stint for the government-controlled news agency, then called AP of Pakistan, asked Sehbai to stop publication of Kamran's story which dwelt on the links of the ISI with the terrorist and the story was intercepted by it. The editor refused to do so. Gondal was not deterred by it and got to the paper's owner who is also the editor-in-chief (apparently the same system prevails in Pakistan) and the owner, Shakil-ur-Rahman, immediately stopped the story from being published in the Urdu paper, *Jang* and he could not do so in the *News* because the editor, the same Sehbai, made himself unavailable. Since the story was published in all editions of the *News,* including its Islamabad and Karachi editions, immediately all government advertising was stopped. Since the government machinery moves a little slowly the Pakistan government issued the orders on February 18. The story was not only published in all editions of the *News* but also in American papers like the *Washington Post* and the *International Herald Tribune* because the American media can save a lot of money by paying extra to a Pakistani Journalist, as to an Indian journalist, because it costs a huge amount to post a full-time American correspondent. It is much cheaper to let a local man do the job. A journalist has to reach a level of competence of course.

On February 22 the proprietor called a meeting at Karachi at 10 p.m. (the Pakistani proprietors prefer such unearthly hour). He was asked to make-up with the Ministry of I and B and ISI to save his job. He did nothing of the kind but the proprietor went to Islamabad and he was apparently told the same thing and the editor, Shaheen Sehbai, took a flight on February 27 to New York to save his life. The paper's government ad revenue (a considerable amount) was then restored and the proprietor went back to his London resort. All Pakistanis of some means go to London and now all Indians in that category move to London where they can enjoy all the comforts and also make some money.

The Times correspondent, Shobha John, asked Sehbai some more questions. This is what he had to say: "The ISI continues to be a major player in domestic politics (its role in foreign policy is too well known to be recalled). It is actively involved in controlling the media. Pearl murder (Daniel Pearl who was kidnapped and killed by the same Omar Sheikh while Musharraf told the US media in Washington that Pearl was alive) has given them more reason to activate the national interest excuse." The editor listed some instances when the Pakistan government in the past harassed him and even arrested him on false charges and its agent pulled guns on his two sons and said that this was a major financial squeeze on what the *News* group claims to the largest financial group (in the media) and followed by demands to sack him and three other senior journalists. On the role of the media under Musharraf, Sehbai said that they would fight back as soon as they see Musharraf lose his grip. Sehbai also told the paper that under Musharraf the elections in October 2002 would be as free as the recently concluded local bodies polls in which the army named candidates for whom the people had to vote and none else was allowed to win. This is the same Musharraf whom the *Times* and some other media praised to the skies when he came to India in 2001 for the Agra summit and said there was more freedom for the media under the Musharraf regime.

Fortunately, under NDA rule in India there is so much freedom for the media that they go to any extent in attacking the government and the *Hindu* community without any cause in particular.

The comments that the paper was partially redeemed was found to be correct because all references to the ISI hand in the episode were scrupulously cut out of the interview. With Siddharth Varadarajan in Pakistan trying to establish good relations with the Musharraf regime this was inevitable. The papers policy also was such that no reference to ISI was permitted. The venom was reserved for internal matters like the NDA government at the centre and the BJP government in Gujarat which was its special target. The Additional Director of Information, Gujarat government, wrote to the paper and it had to publish the letter on March 22, 2002 when the Additional Director contradicted its correspondent's story of March 14.

There was no display "our correspondent replies" or anything of the kind because the correspondent had no ground to stand upon. He had misrepresented and distorted the Chief Minister's statement explaining the sequence of events in the state. Here it is in the Additional Director's own words".. We would like to state that the Gujarat Chief Minister Narendra Modi, as has been clarified more than once, never made the "action reaction" statement attributed to him. Nor did he cite any laws of Newton, which as we all know, refer to the natural universe and not to human society." The paper made no comments on this and simply swallowed it as a deliberate mistake on its part.

Wrongly put[7], his (correspondent) view is that riots are never spontaneous but are always created by interested organisations with government support. "This formulation is nothing but an archtypal conspiracy theory. It leads to patent absurdities —", says the Additional Director's letter. In fact[8], the paper carried the next day the Director's letter contradicting its earlier report of March 3. Why the letter remained a dead letter is a mystery.

The paper carried reports ascribed to Smita Gupta and Rajesh Ramachandran, one of them a trusted man of Siddharth Varadarajan, now happily ensconced in the country of his liking, where Americans are killed at Sunday prayer the government had ordered the staff to vacate the place since American lives are not safe. One of the two correspondents had even tasted victory for Sonia Gandhi, who would be installed in the office of the Prime Minister the moment Vajpayee quits office. All that is wishful thinking and his fancy may be a little too early. The wish of Rajesh Ramachandran was expressed too early as the NDA at its session on March 22, 2002 decided to stay together. To the surprise of some in the media, despite their continuous propaganda and writing highly motivated stories, another smaller party, having in its fold Christian and Muslim members chose to join the NDA. The futility of the media writing elaborate stories seeking to discredit the NDA and the principal constituent, BJP, there are parties which makes the opposite choice. The Indian Federal Democratic Party's merger is an important decision coming as it does at a critical time when the media are at their loudest and the propaganda the most lethal. The combined effect, what with the Ayodhya and Gujarat situation and the continuous blitz of media reports and writings was against the party joining the NDA. The IFDP should not have opted at all for their joining the NDA. The leader of the five—MP party is P.C. Thomas[9] and the group includes Anwarul Haq. The *Times of India* went without the story. It was probably too shocked by the action of the five MPs and did not have the courage to publish such a refutation of its own reports and propaganda.

The development is too big to be ignored by such a big paper for long although it may criticise the development. This is not the only development of its kind. Earlier the Trinamul Congress of West Bengal and the PMK of Tamil Nadu had rejoined the NDA despite the series of blasts fired at the NDA and its constituents, mainly the BJP and its convenor, George Fernandes. *The Hindustan Times* and the *Times of India* are in the forefront of the attacks on the NDA and the opposition parties are always ready to ask the NDA allies to leave the fold. They are not worried that the path advocated by them would be disastrous if adopted by the parties approached. India would be left without a central government and the same Vajpayee would have to be invited willy nilly by the President and there would be fresh election among other things.

The media blitz against the NDA government and the main constituent, the BJP, has continued unabated all the while. *The Times* is the leader of the media campaign against the BJP and the NDA but gets the best of treatment from the government and its agencies and it is the most imitated and quoted as the paper deserves most of time but surely not on all occasions. The paper displays hostility to the Indian government but it is all for special consideration for the Musharraf regime in Pakistan. Now with Siddarth Varadarajan reporting from Pakistan, the *Times* gives the maximum coverage and favourable coverage at that to the Musharraf regime. *The Times* never changes and never flags in support of wrong causes.

The NDA is now strong as it has 315 members in the 544 member Lower House, the 13th Lok Sabha. The Vajpayee regime having completed almost three years of its rule after being sworn in October 1999, is possibly set to complete its five year term and the elections would be held on schedule in 2004, no thanks to the media.

Finally on March 25, the *Times of India* in a story by Rajesh Ramachandran took indirect notice of the IFDP when it described the IDP as "a rag-tag" party and fought shy of the fact there was a Muslim MP in the five man group which joined the NDA and mentioned the Muslim MP among "two others" who had joined the NDA. This speaks volumes of the attitude of the paper which is out to settle scores with the BJP and the NDA, rather than reporting facts. The correspondent and the paper could have asked Thomas why the five MPs made the decision to support the Vajpayee government at a time when the ruling alliance was battling with the twin problem of Gujarat and Ayodhya if it so liked and then played the significance of their action instead of supposing that by their action the joint sitting of the two houses would be able to pass the POTO bill. The paper revealed its real purpose which was to malign the Vajpayee government while playing up the Musharraf regime of Pakistan.

Siddharth Varadarajan, the paper's correspondent now in Pakistan, is busy telling the readers of the paper that Musharraf would survive, he is anti-terrorist and anti-fundamentalist and overall he is a good man and Vajpayee would be well advised to enter into dialogue with him. So, on March 25, 2002 it had to use an AP (American Associated Press) despatch to Pakistan to describe the pain of Christians who gathered on March 24, after the grenade attack on March 17 in their usual church. In the grenade attack five people, including an American woman and her daughter, died and the preacher had to fly out from the US. (How rich the Americans are). The correspondent had no time for filling a story. How many of the paper's readers know of it and are aware of the paper's attitude—double faced as it is?

What the correspondent in Pakistan wanted to achieve was a redemption for Musharraf not news for its own sake or news pure and simple. Unfortunately, the paper thinks it is cut out for much bigger things than news, not realising that news is its bread and butter job for the entire business of the organisation. But in the process it cultivates personal animosities against the Gujarat Chief Minister, for example, whom it tried to cultivate in the beginning for his career but apparently failed in the attempt because it went hammer and tongs for the Chief Minister's ouster when the Gujarat communal cauldron overflowed following the Godhra massacre. The train in question stopped only for five minutes at the Godhra station on February 27, 2002 and nothing of consequence could have happened in those five minutes.

We say this because the paper tried in spite of the first report of the massacre it carried earlier when an unvarnished version was presented, to whitewash the initial crime which could have changed the entire cycle of events in Gujarat. The story in the closing stages of the month of March 2002 in the Ahmedabad edition of the paper, later published by all editions, tries very hard to claim that it was not a well planned attack in which the Pakistani ISI could have played a part. Quite apart from it, the attack was well planned because it was carried out a kilometre away from the main Godhra station by pulling the train stopping chain. What is significant is the attempt on the part of the paper to present the massacre as a reaction, not a well planned action which would justify the communal events which were totally unjustified. You cannot avenge the massacre by starting a chain reaction of a communal nature and justify the killing of innocent citizens.

But this accords with the general approach of the paper, one of hostility to the NDA government which it calls the BJP regime. It invents many names like calling POTO (later turned by the joint sitting of the two houses of Parliament into POTA after it approved POTO overwhelmingly) as the "Terror Law" for two days in its headlines in the Delhi editions front page until the paper was told about the *faux pas*. It wrote an entire story from the opposition's point of view and wrote a special story on it. It took no or little notice of the fact that the AIADMK members voted in favour of POTO as directed by the Chief Minister of Tamil Nadu. It revealed its open pro-Congress bias when it described as the communal government of Vajpayee along with the Narendra Modi government of Gujarat.

The Gujarat situation was overdone and its anti-Modi bias was revealed when it published its editorial attacking

Modi on March 28 and repeated its Newton charge although it carried a contradiction.

The Gujarat situation can be compared with the situation in Bihar when Jawaharlal Nehru had ordered the nation's air force to bomb the Bihar Hindus who were retaliating and when Gandhiji led a mission to Noakhali in East Bengal. That was in 1946 when the Muslim League Chief Minister (then called Prime Minister) called a Direct Action and killed off some 5,000 men at one stroke. Suhrawardy was the CM of United Bengal and ruled from Calcutta (it was yet to be known by its indigenous name of Kolkata) and the chain reaction set off. First the Muslims of East Bengal retaliated when they went berserk and attacked many Hindus in their area and as a reaction of it the Bihar Hindus retaliated by killing off many Muslims. Then Nehru, as Vice President in Gen. Wavell's interim government, used the bombing technique and Gandhiji applied balm to the wounds of the people suffering in Bengal. (Later the people of East Bengal, who were part of Pakistan, revolted against the torture and authoritarianism of the West Pakistan military in 1971, and with the help of the Indian army fought for their independence and won it.)

Gandhiji fought all his life for Hindu Muslim unity and ultimately gave his life for it. He fought against the slaughter of Kolkata Muslims and even fasted for the northern Muslims in Delhi just before his death. What we try to do by recalling the events of the partition and the days before it is to recall the normalcy of the past 50 years and more and say that normalcy in Gujarat can be restored once the daily attacks in the media stop. The media seem to have a vested interest in the Gujarat situation and are not allowing the situation to return to normalcy by keeping up the attacks on the Gujarat CM and the people of the state. Once these stop normalcy can return at once. It is no longer possible to use the air force and there is no Gandhiji who can apply balm at to the afflicted people of the state.

That Narendra Modi is an *obsession* with the *Times* if India will be clear from the following.

"Modi summoned" is the heading of a story in the paper. The story reads as follows:

"New Delhi: The National Commission for Minorities in an emergency meeting on Monday resolved to summon the Gujarat chief secretary and home secretary to appear before it on April 6. According to a statement," both officials have been asked to bring the list of persons who died and those who have been arrested during the riots. The commission has also directed them to apprise them of the measures taken by the state government to stop the violence. "(TNN)"[10]

In the entire story Modi is nowhere mentioned and the paper headlines the story "Modi summoned". Modi is seen everywhere.

Siddharth Varadarajan, now back from Pakistan where he tried his utmost to make Musharraf a popular hero, is engaged in writing on Gujarat from his perch in New Delhi. He has the advantage of the *Hindustan Times* having a similar story written from New Delhi about Gujarat. Vinod Sharma, a Congressman (recall his story about Sonia's "future rally being a huge one) and Siddharth Varadarajan by the same token should be an upcoming Congressman. No wonder both write as the spokesmen of the Congress party.

The situation in Gujarat cannot be described as anything but bad but there is no reason to decry the whole state. The opposition leaders are losing no opportunity to needle the NDA government at the Centre and the media are doing their bit to help them.

We have drawn attention to the communal situation being bad in several Congress ruled states and among other measures to control the Hindus rushing at Muslims and vice versa the enforcement of a fairly prolonged curfew had to be resorted to. The media never takes notice of such things although the agency and even their own reports speak of a bad position. Among the places and towns affected are Akola and Kalyan, near Mumbai, in Maharashtra, and Khandwa in Madhya Pradesh, ruled by the Congress. However, the media noticed Gujarat incidents although the situation in the entire state, barring some areas, is absolutely quiet and normal.

Attention has also been drawn to the principal paper, The *Times of India*, seeing Modi, the Gujarat Chief Minister, everywhere and carrying on a controversy over remarks never made by him. The following letter published in the paper applies mainly to it, although neither the paper nor the writer of the latter names the paper.

Under the title "Media Bias" the letter writer, who used the website of the paper (from *Times of India*.com which also explains why the paper published the letter) the paper published the following letter:

"The allegations that the English media is biased may not be entirely untrue. I have been keenly following events since February 27 (in Gujarat, one should add, and also clarify that on February 27 a mob of Muslims attacked Sabarmati Express and killed by burning 58 persons in Godhra town (a communally sensitive area) when the train stopped. In both the Gujarati media and the English media....I can say, without any bias, that while the vernacular press reported the facts as they were, the English media highlighted a one-sided view which suited their preconceived notions and favoured a particular minority. While one definitely agrees that killing of innocent people must be condemned, irrespective of their religion, fairness demands that no injustice should be done to anybody on the pretext of secularism. —Mihira Patel lycos.com."[11]

Being a Gujarati, as most Patels are, she read both the English media and also the Gujarati media, and was able to make a distinction in their presentation of the tragic events. It is futile to hope that the paper would also make changes in its coverage because it has published the letter criticising its coverage which is highly biased.

All the papers and the electronic media would, however, be sure to come under severe strain if and when the Congress party is back in power. Once in power, the Congress will wield the big stick and remind the media when they marched in protest against the defamation bill when Rajiv Gandhi was Prime Minister. Some well known names in the media came out in protest against the repressive rule of the Rajiv Gandhi and marched from the Boat Club, as it was then customary, all along the Rajpath in 1988-89 and the then Prime Minister was forced to withdraw the measure. That was under a more liberal regime, of Rajiv Gandhi, and not under the totally repressive rule of his mother.

Under the rule of the Congress party, whether it is the more liberal Rajiv Gandhi or his mother Indira Gandhi, who ruled the dictum "no one has credibility", the media have had it. I have considerable experience of functioning under Minister V.C. Shukla, who was notorious during the emergency and my entire career was under the repressive regime of the Congress party except two years and four months when the Janata Party ruled the country and what was triumphantly proclaimed as the return of democracy was in position.

The worst experience was when the Congress party had decided that enough was enough and the time had come to test public opinion when Indira Gandhi came one afternoon to Broadcasting House and announced to the Indian people that she was conducting a Lok Sabha poll in March 1977. The day the radio announcement was made was January 19 when the press censorship was partially lifted and the press media felt as though they has been completely liberated, although the emergency regulations were only off for the purpose of the Lok Sabha elections.

All the same, we at the News Services Division felt that we ought to do our bit. Accordingly, we went ahead (I was then the Director of News Services, a key post in the government and the secret telephone facilities were among my entitlement) and covered the Janata Party, which Indira Gandhi attacked in her election speeches, adequately. We found that the ratio of the Janata Party to the Congress party came to as much as 45 per cent, the Congress party still getting 55 per cent.

This did not satisfy the Congress leaders and the secretary, I and B, as the agent of the party, conveyed this to me. He ordered me to raise the ratio for the Congress Party to 2:1, it being the ratio of the entire opposition, mainly the four party combination of the Janata Party, not to be confused with the later and largely paper organisation of Subramaniam Swamy. Radio as a medium of Mass Communication was of prime importance as there was little or no TV and the only other media were the newspapers[12].

On February 24 the secretary ordered me to raise the

share of the Congress Party to 2:1 but it was changed within a week, on March 3, to 3:4. Even this did not satisfy diehard Congressman and this group included Shukla's brother Shyama Charan Shukla who happened to be the Chief Minister of Madhya Pradesh, a major Congress-ruled state. V.C. Shukla, our boss, had on Indira Gandhi's defeat joined the Janata Dal and was Minister in the breakaway group of 65 Chandra Shekhar members which was sustained in office for four months by Rajiv Gandhi's Congress Party until the elections during which he was assassinated. Shukla later returned to the Congress Party and for a while became Minister.

To resume the narrative, Shyama Charan told his brother that the radio was making the opposition (read Janata Party) points in a "telling manner". He was, in a way, right. Most AIR listeners did not much care for Indira Gandhi's rigmarole but heard carefully the brief points of the Janata leaders carefully. But brother Shyama Charan's complaint was heard in the corridors of power and the secretary ordered me to clear the evening and morning bulletins with him personally and the subsidiary bulletins of 2 p.m. and 6 p.m. with the Additional Secretary, a senior police officer originally, with the instructions that only limited number of Janata Party leaders like Morarji Desai, Jayaprakash himself, Acharya Kripalani and Charan Singh be covered.

The consequence was that the ratio went to the fantastic proportions and eventually rose to 8.5:1 in favour of the Congress Party. Many of the Congress "leaders" who dared not address public meetings were interviewed by AIR correspondents under oral orders. On pain of losing one's job, or being transferred to unknown destinations one had to carry out these orders. When on March 20, the election results were announced we had to mention the Congress party first and in no case were the trends to be announced. A huge crowd waited at the Bangalore station of AIR to the result of Indira Gandhi herself and her son Sanjay Gandhi and they threw the allegations around. In the last stages of the elections, the Minister used his clout to the maximum. There were imaginary attacks on Sanjay and some other congress leaders. We were made to cover all this and Condemn it.

Todays' generation of mediamen know not what they are doing by making the path of the opposition, mainly the Congress Party, easier for it to return to power not knowing the tribulations which the Congress Party is capable of. Today the Prasar Bharati employees even criticise the Vajpayee government and the non-official media are free to do what they like. They can show a photograph of the teacher at an empty class without realising that class before the examinees enter the room is always empty. Respected police officers said on April 18, 2002[13], that as many as 98 per cent of the 10 and 12 class examinees were present to take the examination and one of the papers even said it. So how can the correspondents say that Muslims boycotted the examinations? It would be a severe slap on the face of the Modi government if after it made elaborate police and bus arrangements the response was a total absence of the examinees.

Note that References

1. Read the story, front page in *The Hindustan Times*, Delhi, on March 8, 2002 "HT: Being followed as usual. " The hint in the story is that the *Times of India*, Delhi, engaged the agency ORG-Marg. The vain ego of the paper "as usual" is there in the headline, but it is a fact that the paper imitates the *TOI* in many respects.

2. *The Times of India,* Delhi, October 21, 2001.
3. *The Times of India,* October 21, 2001, Delhi.
4. *The Times of India,* Delhi, October 18, 2000.
5. The author's book, *The Great Divide: Muslim Separatism and Partition,* published by Gyan, Delhi, reproduces a number of articles of the Constitution of the freedom of the religious minorities.
6. *The Times of India,* Delhi, March 18, 2002.
7. *The Times of India,* Delhi, March 22 and 23, 2002.
8. *Ibid.*
9. *Ibid.*
10. *The Hindustan Times,* Delhi, March 24, 2002.
11. *The Times of India,* April 2, 2002, Delhi edition.
12. "Radio: exploitation for Congress during Election" was the name of a pamphlet brought out those days, being my testimony before the Justice Shah Commission of Inquiry which was extensively covered by all the media. Justice Shah was a retired Chief Justice of India and was conduction an inquiry into the excesses of the emergency.
13. See the *Hindustan Times* and *The Times of India,* Delhi, for the empty class photograph, April 19, 2002.

Five

Non-News Becomes News

It is far from surprising that when the guiding principle is to play up sensation, non-news becomes news because the criterion is what yields a sensational story, not what constitutes news—the truth. Thus, the front page is packed with items which in the old days would go in an inside page, if at all. Gossipy stories, news analysis and what are essentially features now adorn many dailies front pages which in the bygone days would have been consigned to an inside page. Such is the perverted sense of importance that often sports stories come on the front page and some well regulated media imitate the practice, because they find that the circulation level of the more 'advanced' dailies have not fallen. The ABC (Audit Bureau of Circulation) only does a chartered accountant's job. Perhaps it would now attempt a real newsman's job and find out what news stories are featured on the first pages.

The busy urban reader has time only for the headlines and could later in the evening look to the details behind the headlines. In the evening hours nowadays there is the attraction of the medium of TV and some of the channels also carry news—there are some channels which exclusively deal in news with a handful or a lot of ads thrown in. They are also catering to the same clientele as are the newspapers and there is a lot of give and take between them. If an enterprising newspaper has done a good story you can be sure that this is covered in the visual and audio medium of the TV channels and *vice versa*, that is, if the TV news channels have done a good story overnight the newspapers can be expected to follow its lead.

In the year 2000, when Parliament was entering its second week of adjournment, after the two houses were daily adjourned over non-issues (nobody had the time to go into the why of the adjournment), the leading paper, *The Times of India,* asked the question "Did Vajpayee sing the VHP tune[1]?" in the lead story on the front page. The story was far from convincing and the question mark was used by the paper in the customary way. It is a handy device and a tricky innovation. Because the media escape the responsibility when questions are asked about their credibility and they are able to project something which sells. Other examples (a classical one) can be cited. There is the famous one "Are the American media free?" In October 2001, Vajpayee did not sing any tune except the one of the NDA which rules the country from October 1999. *The Times,* like many news media of the print and electronic variety, have tried often to topple Vajpayee but alas they have not succeeded in the effort. Good effort?, as the TV commentators say when a fielder tries to stop a ball and fails in preventing it from crossing the boundary.

The second lead on the same day, "NDA awaits decision in nonexistent case" could have been a feature on an inside page, possibly with a front page indicator. The main news, for the inquisitive reader, was given in box item, what happened or failed to happen in the two houses of Parliament on the day. It is quite clear that the Congress party and some others in the opposition, were totally excused for holding up the proceedings for which they were apparently rewarded by the voters in the four state elections in February 2002.

Who says the media do not play their part in politics? Instead of taking the Congress party and others to task, the media highlight the "achievement" of the party "Deadlock over who gets to speak first—Congress kersists with demand for debate on chargesheeted ministers[2]". *The Indian Express* has the headline—the longest, "PM's mandir heat puts his government in deep freeze—caught in Parliament logjam are crucial economic bills", if you can make some sense of it. The paper also endorses the Congress party's tactics in holding up the proceedings. Every session of Parliament the party finds some cause to hold up the proceedings of the two houses and the media, with some exceptions, just enjoy the situation.

The beauty of headlines would be forgotten soon as the newspapers become history. Bansi Lal, former Chief Minister of Haryana and the Defence Minister of Indira Gandhi during her unpopular emergency rule, used to contemptuously refer to the *"raddi"* of the newspapers, presumably alluding to the resale value of the old newspapers which fetch a good price in India. This does not prevent a deskman from attaching value to his headlines. Some newspapers even employ Hindi words for their headlines, as for example *The Times of India* which ironically calls its Hindi newspaper *The "Navbharat Times"*.

The smart deskman always headlines the news smartly and he goes up in the estimate of those who decide his promotion and posting. But if the source itself is corrupted how will the product (the headline) be? When the sensation is the ultimate goal truth suffers at the alter of a smart paper.

Madhu Dandavate, a veteran former parliamentarian and former Finance Minister in the V.P. Singh government says that there are ways of criticising the government by the opposition parties (the media call it 'flaying') if only the houses are allowed to function[3]. Many mediamen and women are fond of believing that they are secular and liberal and are entitled to their views. But they should have a commitment to truth and must report facts in their newspapers and TV channels. Parliament is the largest pillar of Indian democracy and if it is subject to the game of adjournment after adjournment there is something fundamentally wrong in the process somewhere. Press is sometimes referred to as the fourth estate and although there is no provision in the Constitution for it is read by millions of people everyday and has a duty to the people.

Under the Constitution, there is the freedom of expression which is a fundamental right and this includes the guarantee for freedom of the press[4]. But all rights include corresponding duties and there is such a thing as commitment to values which should be uppermost when such issues are debated in Parliament. But if the two houses are not allowed to function at all what becomes of our democracy? It is hardly relevant that the Prime Minister said something on Ayodhya but the issue must be debated and the party spokesman must have their say. The opposition parties know that as long as the NDA has a majority in the Lok Sabha it will throw out any of the motions they bring up in the debate. But what about the upper house where it does not enjoy the same privilege?

And the NDA is after all human. There is hope eternal in the human breast and Sonia Gandhi, once bitten is not shy or wary of trying again for the coveted post which her husband once occupied with distinction in the first few months and later in embarrassment for a long time. Each time, the opposition parties try for the job for Sonia, the media are ready to fight for her, some just for their own sake, some for the opposition's same, soke for the fun it involves and some because it is fashionable. The media are prone to forget, and none of them know very well, that each time the opposition parties come out to oppose the NDA they do it politically and not because they feel it that way. The media wittingly or unwittingly play into the hands of the opposition parties when they play up with aplomb the Vajpayee government's problems. There is thus a link between the media and the political parties, much more than what the media imagine. They are fully exploited by the political parties of the opposition.

Whether it is Ayodhya or the budget of the Union government, or anything else, the media are always there to do the bidding of the opposition parties and they pretend that they are only doing their duty as media. Just imagine the Times of India highlighting the point in the Supreme Court interim order in March 2002 that the Attorney General made a prayer on behalf of the government that symbolic Bhoomi Puja be allowed. What the Attorney General said, as he explained to the media at which the paper's representative must have been present, was that he was giving his own interpretation of the court's 1994 judgment. He said that he had filed no affidavit on the subject before the court's three judge bench.

The publication on the front page of the paper of a colour picture of Aslam Bhure Khan is not to its credit as a news media but its projection of itself as a protester of minorities in India (which accords with its pro-Pakistan approach). As usual in playing up the opposition's point of view it subtly displays its preference for Congress leader Sonia Gandhi as Prime Minister. What the media did on this occasion was a faint imitation of the paper but it must be said that some dailies acknowledge that Prime Minister Vajpayee was in a win situation.

On the subject of holding up the proceedings of the two houses, we have to add that the convention of not entering the well of the Lok Sabha, in the absence of the Speaker, G.M.C. Balayogi, who called all the party leaders and got their approval at the special meeting, was ignored after his death in a helicopter accident. How—one need not ask, but ignored it was, and, as usual, Raghuvans Prasad of the RJD was among them. He was the loudest, as always, utilising his lung power to the utmost and the media were there to demonstrate that they are interested in sensation not truth. Sections of the media also point out the differences in the opposition parties but on this occasion there were not many or any and they are generally aware that they like political parties, are pointing this out as part of their general coverage.

People like Raghvans Prasad and others who act as their party spokesmen or musclemen think that Parliament is a good target and a good stick to beat the government with. They should be asked what the difference was between postmen who were on strike in 2000 and the autorickshaw men and cabbies who are on strike off and on in Delhi and MPs who have to raise their voices to shout slogans and come out of their seats and enter the prohibited well?

The Statesman[6] of Calcutta and Delhi, one of the exceptional papers to comment on the subject, said that postmen need not be condemned. It said in an editorial: "Why condemn postmen when parliamentarians show no better sense of responsibility? Nearly half this Parliament's session (winter session, 2000) has been lost in the 'strike' over Ayodhya and such discussions as are going on now are mostly centred round the same topic, with the NDA allies doing analysis of the Prime Minister's statements and the Opposition discovering grand conspiracies. Lost in this din is not only legislative decorum but important legislative business."

What we said in an earlier chapter where we quoted a media friendly Congress party MP, about the media's approach to the frequent holdups of the proceeding of the two houses of Parliament, should be linked up here. The Congress party has apparently thrived on its strategy which is not good for the future of Indian democracy and the sooner the BJP gives up its association with religion and emerges as the sole spokesman of the middle classes, the better for democracy. As for Raghuvans Prasad, the less said the better for Indian democracy because those who elected him to the house, and the media who project him repeatedly, must be considering it a special virtue to disturb the proceedings of the Lok Sabha, Raghuvans's own house.

For example, the RJD and the Samajwadi party prevented consideration of the Women's reservations bill in the December 2000 session of Parliament when the loud shouting Raghuvans Prasad was prominent in disrupting the proceedings and preventing the bill's consideration. The same two parties had tried to prevent introduction of the bill earlier. It was brought up when two days remained for the session to end and why the NDA government brought it up so late remains a mystery. Be that as it may, the RJD and the Samajwadi Party knew that they did not have the required strength in the house to vote it out. As the Samajwadi Party leader, Mulayam Singh Yadav, said, as he often does, the bill would not be allowed to be passed and the two parties got the House adjourned by the partymen entering the well of the house and making all kinds of noises to disrupt the proceedings.

The media who are a party to the whole episode

behaved in the usual method of preferring sensation to truth. They cannot get away by blaming this party or that, as is their wont, when the time comes to analyse the session because they give prominence to Raghuvans Prasad and people of his ilk and thus cater to his ego and thereby his acceptability to his electorate. If the media had condemned his disruptive tactics, the BJP, as alleged by some media, would have to vote as a party or be exposed before the house as "opposing" the bill as alleged by some media.

Members of the two parties resorted to extra-constitutional methods and prevented passage of the bill. The minority view prevailed, with the connivance and collaboration of the media (which includes electronic media and even the official media like Doordarshan and AIR). Such is the destructive power of the media.

As usual, the media are too afraid of the organised unions and dare not say a word about their activities. This became evident once again when *The Times of India,* in a front page story "the strike that fizzled out", the paper blamed everyone save the unions which inspired and led the strike. The story laid blame at the doors of the government, which must be blamed if the unions are also reproached, the postal department, which means the government, not the employees or the unions. The unions are too powerful, more than the media, and the courts are always to be eulogised, except when Arundhati Roy gets involved. The paper sheds crocodile tears for the common users and conducted a so-called poll without the readers of the paper being bothered. They are called Delhi-ites but the real readers of the paper were never involved in the exercise. The paper means perhaps the website owners when it says its readers but they were not much affected by the strike, using as they do couriers and E-mail services, but the real users were the urban middle class and the rural areas who heaved a sigh of relief when the strike ended.

The media have demonstrated more than once that they will never rub the unions on the wrong side because of their strength and do not wish to take them on. Many of the media, like *The Statesman* in Calcutta and *The Times of India,* Bombay (now Mumbai), were British owned and Indian interests took them over when the British were leaving. During the freedom struggle the papers called Mahatma Gandhi as "Mr Gandhi" and now perhaps *The Times* would call the Father of the Nation just Gandhi. In the British days, however, they were not afraid of the unions as they are now today, although it must be acknowledged that *The Statesman* displays unique candour and it would not mind calling a spade a spade.

The Times of India in an effort to appear different from its rivals termed the two-day strike of the autorickshaws and taxis in the capital as "indefinite", not realising that the great inconvenience is caused by prolonging the strike. The readers often are taken in by the crocodile tears shed by the paper. and fear is their (the paper's and the media's) main weapon in the war and chaos is what they (the people) fear most. The media thrive on fear which is what is seen when the VHP (Vishwa Hindu Parishad) proclaims a face-saving device in March 2002. They play up to the threats of the VHP while they give full coverage to the opposition parties and the so-called minority leaders, by which the media recognise the Muslims and those who claim to speak in their name.

The people are the real targets when the unions call frequent strikes in public utilities like banks, electricity and related trades, autos and taxis and buses and all others affected what are known as the general public. The government are generally the owners (except such trades as autos and taxis which are the exclusive preserve of the private sector) and the people suffer at the hands of the unions who enforce the strikes. When the Kerala and some other high courts called the Bandhs (work stoppages) as illegal some, media supported the courts but the vast majority kept quiet and some even questioned the violation of the people's democratic rights. Now that the Congress government in Kerala was affected by a month long strike of teachers and government employees the media after reporting the strike extensively revel in the strike achieving[6] "nothing'.

The media, in their general attitude, display considerable concern for the welfare of the people but they are more interested in portraying the picture of chaos which results when public utility men go on strike. They think that their purpose will be served if the chaos rules in the country resulting from frequent strikes. They forget that their purpose would be better served by everything done according to plan. When the bundles of the print media move without hindrance at the bus terminals and railway stations and there is no stoppage of any kind (including the effort by *The Times of India* to stop *The Hindustan Times* bundles, as the Latter complained) the time is never out of joints for the media. But what of the chaos which the media love to portray?

Here they follow the practice they love, the Parliament hold-up which the Congress party and others in the opposition resort to often. But the parliamentary holdup are not to be compared with the oft-resorted strikes by Communist-inspired unions which have a highly motivated political purpose in mind. Except the three states of West Bengal, Kerala and Tripura they have no other state in the country where they have any stronghold. In the assembly election in Kerala in 2001, the Congress party came to power which they had lost to the CPIM, as the spearhead of the Left movement. So musical chairs are played in the states of Kerala and Tripura and would have been extended to West Bengal also in 2001 if Mamata Banerjee had not teamed up with the Congress and kept its alliance with the NDA to which she returned later after the elections.

Without power in the state of Kerala they resort to strikes or support strikes like the strike of teachers and government employees. That is how they hope to come back to power in Kerala. They fool the Italian lady who is chief of the Congress party by virtue of being the widow of the late Prime Minister who was also Congress President during the entire period when he was Prime Minister and even after he had to give up that position because the BJP-supported V.P. Singh government came to power in November-December 1989 and until his tragic death. Sonia is fooled because as the Congress President she wants more states to be under her rule, in Delhi she is subject to CPIM propaganda and is also apparently supportive of the CPIM-dominated People's Front.

Some media support the Congress party because they are habituated to do so and some support it because they like the Congress President. This is the media's tribute to foreigners in reverse gear. It may be a far cry for Sonia to be Prime Minister, if at all, but what does it matter if there is a small investment for the future and the BJP-led NDA is not likely to last long, as the media (or a section of them) think.

That is how the media vision is, narrow and stilted. The media are too clever by half, as the saying goes. Some people feel that a particular paper has gone down in its stand, but we feel that the disease is affecting the whole range of them and there is something wrong with the entire system. When, for example, an interview is conducted by the electronic media and what is known as grilling is reduced to taking down on the voice camera the interviewee's statement against the government and later on it is described as "grilling" we look ridiculous and have to hang our heads in shame. Is this really "grilling"? Or is it the satisfaction of the reporter that he or she has an interview with a celebrity.

In contrasting style are the headings and treatment of the story relating to the Supreme Court's interim order on the VHP and Ramajanmabhoomi Nyas of the Mahant Ramchandra Paramhans's and the VHP's plans to build the temple at Ayodhya at a site a little away from the site of the disputed structure where the Babri Masjid once stood. The Supreme Court on March 13, 2002 had said in its order that no puja of any kind could be performed on the disputed land nor could it be performed on the undisputed land acquired by the government. The court had been approached by litigant Bhure Khan. We have chosen *the Hindu,* known for its sober treatment and headings *The Hindustan Times* which stood somewhat halfway and the leading paper, *The Times of India,* known to sensationalise news.

On March 15, the day the Mahant threatened to burn himself if he was not allowed to perform the puja, *The Hindu* heading was "security blanket over Ayodhya as VHP is firm on Shiladan." The Shilas are carved stones which would be erected in the temple when it is constructed but the Mahant wanted to make a *dan* (gift) of them to mark the beginning of the temple construction in defiance of the apex court's order. *The Hindustan Times* headlined the news as follows: "VHP vows to go ahead" and to clarify the heading it added "Puja or death: Paramhans". *The Times of India* headline read 'Shiladaan' or suicide, threatens mahant" and in subtitles it said "VHP defiant, RSS unhelpful, Government desperate".

The Hindu had its correspondent, Anjali Mody in Ayodhya proper, *The Hindustan Times* a two town story, from Ayodhya and New Delhi and *The Times* had, one from Ayodhya and one from New Delhi. Now let us see how the three papers had the news on March 16, the day following the threat of the over 90 years old Mahant to court death (at first he had said that he would court arrest). On March 15 itself, by noon, he had changed his mind and like the inflated baloon everything was peaceful throughout the country. The headings of three papers were as follows: "Central emissary receives 'shila' " and in a superscribed heading *The Hindu* added: 'Ceremony away from acquired land: Ayodhya breathes easy". *The Hindustan Times* heading ran: "Low-key shila daan, quiet Puja" which conveyed everything the paper wanted to say. The Times heading ran: "Ayodhya face-off ends in whimper".

The Hindu headings are factual but its 16th March heading did not convey the why of the peaceful atmosphere prevailing all over the country, which was because of the climb down by the Mahant. *The Hindustan Times* had to put its favourite Sonia Gandhi on the front page and *The Hindu* had its commitment to Narasimha Rao who was acquitted by the Delhi High Court the same day. *The Times* predicament can be well realised because it had built up the tempo (look at the heading on Gujarat -'fireworks') and it was sorely disappointed at the peaceful end to the whole episode, which is why it talked of a whimper. Narasimha Rao's acquittal deserved a place on the front page but on a day like this it did not require a second lead to do justice to the story as *The Hindu* gave.

Far from analysing the causes for the Mahant to give up his threat to end his life, *The Times* indulged its favourite 'caste card' and the invisible hand of the ISI. *The Hindustan Times* made an effort on an inside page to find out who persuaded the Mahant to give up his plans under the heading "How the VHP was brought around". Harish Khare attempts a story in *The Hindu* in which he gives much of the credit to the Prime Minister and some credit to the Home Minister for persuading the Mahant. The PM never spoke to the Mahant.

As is the custom, the papers wrote editorials on the event or non-event, and while the editorials of *The Hindustan Times* and *The Hindu* were on expected lines *The Times* edit (the paper is fond of the word) pontificated as usual. While praising the court, so as not to fall foul, the paper talked of everything under the sun. The real story was given under its lead heading when the whole episode ended, according to it, in whimper. Much to its chagrin, there were no stories of violence and its usual quota of horror stories would have to be fulfilled some other way. It should have come out with the Vajpayee government having the courage to arrest in UP some of the top leaders of the VHP who wanted to reach Ayodhya somehow on March 15 and for its action of unprecedented show of strength in deploying large numbers of paramilitary forces in Ayodhya, where the police outnumbered VHP men, and similar actions of the government. Under the liberal regime of Vajpayee, the paper attacked the government as always, when it caved in to the emergency rules of Indira Gandhi, in fact, among the first papers to do so. Exploit the government rules and its liberal attitude to the utmost and cave in when, on the impossible return of the Congress to power, it waves a stick at the media.

The media should thank their stars that there is a government in power at the Centre which does not wield the stick at all. It, of course, utilises the services of its various agencies of publicity and there, we are afraid, a big cut was expected as media reports averred. We have a media which always strive to destroy what the people of India built and political parties which seek to oust the Vajpayee government and their principal occupation is to put the Italian lady in the Prime Minister's office. The General Secretary of the CPIM, the busybody Harkrishan Singh Surjeet, had once a one-point programme, put Sonia in the Prime Minister's position. Many think that the same continued to be his programme even now although officially he is connected with the People's Front.

Our comments on the Sunday papers should be recalled because the Sunday following the Ayodhya incident, which took place on Friday March 15, was utilised by a number of media to blame the Hindu Community and heap all blame on it for Ayodhya and Gujarat.

We have to recall the liberal approach of the Vajpayee government to contrast it with the stick-wielding Congress rule. Because of my close connection with the media units of the I and B ministry, during the Congress regime, I have vivid memories of the terror which prevailed during Indira Gandhi's emergency rule and later when she relaxed the emergency and called for general elections and the official media had no respite.

During the elections to the Lok Sabha incalculable harm was done to the credibility of AIR news. I happened to be the Director of News of AIR which enjoyed monopoly of spot and instantaneous news which Indira Gandhi was well aware and tried to control through the well-oiled I and B ministry and Minister Shukla. He like left the Congress party and even became a Minister in Chandrashekhar's breakaway government later to sheepishly walk back to the Congress party.

At the time of the Lok Sabha elections (and even much later when the satellite TV arrived in early nineties) the Radio was the only means of mass communication which many people listened to despite its many failings. As I said before the Shah Commission of Inquiry into the excesses committed during the Emergency[7] "The AIR news broadcasts during the Lok Sabha Election campaign were subjected to unprecedented pressures and the most cynical and blatant manipulations in the interest of the ruling Congress party. By then, the censorship had been relaxed and most of the newspapers were acting once more as members of a free press but not AIR. Nevertheless on our own we tried to restore the credibility....". Following the announcement of the Lok Sabha elections on January 18, 1977, we succeeded to bring balance in the bulletins. The coming together of the four principal parties to form the Janata Party (not to be mistaken with Subramaniam Swamy's paper organisation) was noticed with prominence. Likewise, the Janata Party manifesto was given prominent coverage in the AIR bulletins.

These and other events connected with the Janata Party did not go well with the leaders of the Congress Party and as the agent of the party the Secretary of the I and B ministry conveyed this to me and ordered that the

Congress Party be given more prominence (we had managed a ratio of 55 to 45 per cent) and now the coverage of Congress Party was to be 2:1, 1 being the fate of the entire opposition, mainly the Janata Party which Indira Gandhi attacked in her election speeches. This was the order on February 24, elections were due to be held on March 19, 1977, and the complaint was that AIR was being unnecessarily "fair" to the opposition. This order was orally passed on February 24 but soon the ratio in favour of the Congress Party was raised on March 3 to 3:1.

Even this did not satisfy the diehard Congressmen, including Shukla's brother who happened to be the Chief Minister of a major state like Madhya Pradesh. He said that the opposition points were made "in a telling manner". Most listeners did not care for the rigmarole of Indira Gandhi but listened carefully to the brief but telling points of the Janata Party leaders. So, there were orders of the Secretary that I should clear the bulletins (morning and evening) with him personally and with the Additional Secretary, a senior police officer, the day and the early evening bulletins. The ratio thus went to the fantastic proportion of 8.5:1, in favour of the Congress Party. Many of its "leaders" who dare not address any meetings were interviewed by AIR correspondents (according to the Secretary's orders) to increase the Congress huge share and to make it look that they were canvassing for their party, not Indira Gandhi alone, while only chosen leaders of the Janata Party were mentioned by name. Others were simply ignored.

When the election results were announced on March 20, the orders were that no trends were to be broadcast, the Congress Party was to be mentioned first, and so on. Of course, on March 21 the Secretary was in no mood to listen to the defeat of the Congress Party and its leaders including Indira Gandhi herself and her son Sanjay Gandhi, and we did our newsman's duty. The Congress Party and Minister Shukla resorted to many tricks including a fake attack on Sanjay Gandhi for which the Minister rang up the DG, AIR, IST 1 a.m. on March 15 to give instructions (the DG had no role in the bulletins but the Minister rang him up) as to how the bulletins should play up the incident and how various Congress leaders were to be interviewed and our correspondents were to be utilised for the purpose.

This was blatant misuse of the radio for a party purpose and it so happened that the party was in power. Today, as Prasar Bharati employees, AIR and Doordarshan reporters even criticise the government while they can and often are transferred to media which are directly under the government. Do the media, in the print variety and electronic channels, know it? Do they care to know it while they freely attack the Vajpayee government at the Centre and the Narendra Modi government in Gujarat without the least mention of the Godhra attack in which 58 people were killed. Has the Narendra Modi government done any harm to *The Times of India* edition at Ahmedabad or *The Indian Express* editions at Ahmedabad and Baroda. Now *The Times* has also a Baroda edition of the paper and we should mention it lest the growing empire feels ignored (Vadodara and Baroda are one and the same). The instances of any bias should be brought and the Godhra tragedy should be prominently mentioned. Instead we have a parrot like repetition that Modi is an RSS man, as though the being in the RSS once was stigma for life without knowing that diehard Muslims have paid tributes to the RSS for giving a decent burial to the Muslims killed (along with Hindus who were cleaned) when a Saudi Arabian plane collided with another aircraft and killed some people in Haryana.

The paper attributed to Modi something which he never uttered, specially about Newton's law that any action produces a reaction referring to the Godhra incident causing a natural reaction throughout Gujarat. We have said before that its Delhi edition never mentioned in its headlines that Ahmedabad was now peaceful although the story said so. The readers should be aware that the previous Congress government had given land to the Ahmedabad edition of the paper. It made fun of Modi when he won convincingly the by-election to the Gujarat assembly from Rajkot by mentioning in its headline "Modi hangs on". At first its Ahmedabad edition made a wrong forecast of the constituency from which Modi was to contest. The paper's grudge against Modi was apparent. What happened in Gujarat does not merit anything then except strong condemnation but the media trying to belittle and forget the Godhra episode has to be pointed out.

Almost all prominent papers swallowed the insults in the Emergency and only *The Indian Express* protested. We know how *The Times* virtually pocketed the many insults during the Emergency but we also know that it loves the Congress Party and its Italian leader Sonia and would like to see her at the helm in India. How the Congress dealt with the media we have dealt with by quoting chapter and verse. The return of the stick-wielding regime would be heralded in what manner we do not know, but it is certain that the Congress rule would be much worse.

Let the media, particularly the print media, point out the Ayodhya incident if any harassment and violence is caused to the minorities but the climate of anti-BJP and anti-Vajpayee reports and the totally unjustified playing up of the VHP and the Ramjanmabhoomi Nyas must stop. All reports must be done with a balance of mind and nothing should be done to provoke the elements ready to jump into the fray. In the name of reporting the "facts", what we now see is exaggeration, distortion and misrepresentation and creating an anti-minority atmosphere with the object of provoking more incidents so that a continuous supply of stories of tension and actual violence is maintained. "Whimper" is specially relevant in this context.

Notes and References

1. *The Times of India,* December 12, 2000, Delhi edition.
2. *The Hindustan Times, Indian Express* and *The Times of India,* Delhi, December 12, 2000.
3. "Ayodhya issue shows collapse of Parliament's authority" *The Hindustan Times,* Delhi, Dec. 13, 2000.
4. See "Press in India since 1955" by the author, Publications Division Delhi.
5. "SC Rejects Govt's Prayer for Puja," *The Times of India,* Delhi, March 14, 2002.
6. "House Training: MPs must be forced to behave", *The Statesman,* Delhi December 18, 2000.
7. "Radio Exploitation for Congress during election", a pamphlet brought out containing my testimony. Justice J.C. Shah, a retired Chief Justice of India, was appointed by the government of India to inquire into the excesses of the Emergency in 1977-78.

Six

Electronic Media's Role

When we talk of the electronic media, two things have to be remembered—that there are numerous satellite channels in India and a large number of them are foreign. Thus, the bilingual New Delhi TV (NDTV) is linked with the Star TV network which is foreign. Rupert Murdoch is Australian by birth and American by adoption. He is thus cent per cent foreign but the Star Plus channel, an entertainment channel, is lauded to the skies by many in the print media who fail to point out that the profit earned by Murdoch goes abroad. No channel which is exclusively devoted to news and current affairs is happily foreign. The only exclusive channel *Aaj Tak* is completely Indian. Because it is watched by a large number of people it is successful in winning the confidence of the advertisers or a series of ads and commercial messages in the form of news. Aaj Tak was originally on Doordarshan's Metro channel when it did not get the flurry of ads that it now gets. Since the Sony (foreign) channel gets business even while its signal is not entirely steady, (as Doordarshan's signal is) the *Aaj Tak* had for a considerable time the problem of its signal not being steady and yet it attracted a lot of business. Now happily its satellite signal has stabilised.

The print media makes plenty of noise over the possible entry of foreign capital in the media but are gaily unaware or pretend to be unaware of the presence of foreign TV being beamed into India and they are encouraging the foreign media in TV by praising their programmes.

If exaggeration and sensationalism is the soul of the print media, the electronic media are not far behind. In fact, they have no time for analysis. They are so much concerned with the coverage of the minute-to-minute developments that they forget the main job of the media which is, apart from the factual coverage, giving the viewers an insight into the developments so that the viewers get a genuine satisfaction from watching the channel. The print media criticise in season and out of season, the government where they follow the lead of the opposition parties who are really interested in toppling the NDA in power and then fight among themselves for the Prime Ministership, the media criticise the opposition parties, except their favourite party, the industry and agriculturists, students and all classes and categories except the unions which are left to fend for themselves. As it is, the media in general are too afraid of the unions and their power behind them, the organised labour force.

Once an editor described India as "disaster country" when two foreign planes collided on Indian soil. The paper was *The Indian Express* which as we have observed is the only real all-India paper as it covers the whole of India except the east. The comment came from no less a person than the editor himself and he was angry because the Indian staff did not, as alleged by the editor, properly guide the colliding planes. The comment and the event are both forgotten but the tendency of the media to sit in judgement over alleged disasters to aircrafts and trains persists. Due to hardship many lovers of ease may not avail of the facility of air-conditioned travel on some of the important trains but that cannot be put down to media criticism of the railways.

It is not our intention to stop the flow of criticism but to point out the false and uphold the genuine. All over the world planes and trains go down and in the most sophisticated country they fall to the ground in the most dramatic circumstances. In November 2001, the American Airlines plane crashed soon after takeoff from New York and almost every day or on alternate days there is a fairly big air or train disaster in the world but any air crash or train derailment in India is hounded upon by the media and treated as a disaster. They are usually ignorant of the rules and they religiously proclaim that a statutory inquiry is to be held into a certain rail accident. Now the rules require that every railway accident of serious nature is statutorily inquired into by the Commissioner of Railway Safety who is senior railwayman but under the Communications Ministry to ensure objectivity in the matter.

There is real rush for tickets and the Railways resort to the Tatkal Seva and similar devices but are not able to put down corruption yet. The media should be investigating this aspect but the PR man or woman ensures by his good PR that no investigation is made. This is a media failure, the most common one, but no attempt has been made by either the print media or the electronic media to cover the phenomenon of ticket booking, ticketless travel, the headquarters quota release and the various manipulation at the seat of Railway Ministers office where any number of people try to use their influence. Lakhs of people are genuinely interested in the investigation but the media have their priorities in which there is no place for any suggestions.

Another case of real concern for the many traveller is the accident which occurs almost invariably by the overspeeding of the drivers of buses and some private cars in crossing the unmanned railway crossings. All railways in the world have them and the bus drivers who use them are trained to look out for trains before going across the rail line but egged on as they are they forget their primary duty to look after their passenger. The media are too preoccupied with their problems but it should be their concern to save human lives which are lost when a bus or a private car runs into a fast moving train.

The media find the railways too easy a victim when they blame the railway administration for the accident when they must know that a train in motion cannot be stopped at once as the bus or car can. The drivers have to be careful and the conductors have to be active if there is awareness that the drivers and conductors have a duty to perform. In all good and concerned lands the bus driver stops at an unmanned railway crossing, the conductor gets down to look for trains and then only the bus proceeds forward after checking the train movements. But invariably, the media blame the railways for the accident and thus encourage the laxity of the bus drivers and conductors.

About egging on there is no dearth of people who encourage the driver to ignore the consequences of their own actions and of the drivers who they goad to go ahead and ignore the common sense rule that safety of passengers is their paramount responsibility. Often the buses are carrying wedding parties and the busy bodies among the parties sit next to the driver and provoke him to drive recklessly.

If the print media are interested in self-glorification there is no paucity of the electronic media (the TV channels) in imitating them. Let us begin with the *Aaj Tak* channel which is competently run and attracts the maximum number of commercial messages for a purely news channel.

In the United States many TV stations are attached to the newspapers and there is a genuine relationship of closeness between the two. Similarly in India the *India Today* group has sponsored the *Aaj Tak* channel. Most print media have not yet entered the TV field, although *The Times of India* has a variety of business interests, mainly in the entertainment field. May be, one of these days, you would find a TV channel linked to a paper. The Sahara, on the other hand, had a TV concern and then a paper, the *Rashtriya Sahara*. One can say that the TV channel business is yet to attract the print media but a surprise could be expected.

The *Aaj Tak* is, however, not free from the virus of exaggeration. It is, of course, not concerned in competition with any channel but is, of course, conscious of the competing channels like the NDTV which has teamed up with the foreign channel of Star TV and with the Zee news channel which is a genuine news and current affairs channel. But as we said, even the *Aaj Tak* is not free of the exaggeration problem. If the situation in Gujarat is seen to be the target of the opposition in the Lok Sabha and the Rajya Sabha, the Ahmedabad correspondent is alerted and he keeps on sitting in the police control room and his reports are seen in the context of the opposition criticism. Thus, there is exaggeration but the channel refrains from the art of distortion.

The sensation bug bites the TV channel as much as some media but the channel tries to avoid the situation when its sensationalism hurts the viewers. It made no attempt to explain its so-called exit polls in the recent state assembly elections in 2002 when it made wrong predictions. It had no option except to swallow the whole mistake. It fails to avoid its mistake when the headline news is not given any long or no treatment in the bulletin as all headline news is expected to. The channel tries to raise the curiosity of its readers but the curiosity is never satisfied. This is a real failure and the sooner it is cured the better.

It is the answer to many viewers urge to avoid looking at the morning paper because the viewer does not want to waste too much time and resources running after the news in the newspaper. Looking at the channel news is satisfying and the viewers, many of them busy people, do not feel the need to buy a newspaper. It is unique in the sense that the channel has a genuine interest at news, presentation and is not an adjunct of an entertainment channel. The Zee news channel is an extension of a highly successful entertainment channel. Like the Zee news the *Aaj Tak* channel is entirely Hindi while the NDTV, which is linked to Star, is bilingual both in English and Hindi. Why the channel fights shy of the Metro connection is beyond the imagination of many.

Many are the advantages of the link being cut off and of the separation of the two. Now apart from being a separate channel and much larger revenues, it has started to look outside and it covered the US-Afghan war in a remarkable manner. The sports should be covered more elaborately than at present because the viewers demand the sport stories in a colourful sweep, not as an appendage as at present. A time may come when a separate channel would be in existence for sports news and the *Aaj Tak* will have to guard against the possibility. There is indeed scope for a separate sports channel to cover the main national events and even bid for international events and yet provide news relating to sports on a fixed point schedule. In the media world one has to keep abreast of all the developments and be conscious of the future possibilities also.

The pressures exerted on the media for coverage of

self and the point of view represented by one is well known. We do not know whether the *Aaj Tak* channel covered Dungarpur in defence of the anti-Indian bias openly displayed by Mike Deness was an act of folly or because of the pressure of Dungarpur but surely it was ill-advised and the coverage was totally unnecessary. The print media may succumb to pressure specially the agency covering Dungarpur but the worth or worthlessness of people like Dungarpur should be known to everyone.

These are pitfalls of the media. But the need for an elaborate sports coverage cannot be overemphasised if the channel is to hold viewer interest. The announcement of the Indian cricket team to tour West Indies was a test case for the media. The interest in the announcement was not only whether Dinesh Mongia would find a place in it but in the overall composition of the team. So, it was necessary for the channel to give the entire team after the intro in including Dinesh Mongia and the fact that some players had staged a comeback in the team after they were dropped for the Zimbabwe tour.

The excuse that Doordarshan news had done so should not be cited in support. Doordarshan dealt with it as if the interest was confined to Dinesh Mongia and Yuvraj Singh. While the two had done tremendously well in the recent one-day series against Zimbabwe, the national channel forgot that a test team is selected on different grounds. Its disposal of the item in its main news bulletin was snappy in the extreme and so in the earlier bulletins.

But the Doordarshan bulletins are invariably more newsy than any other bulletins from any private channels who attract commercial ads all the same. It may be because of internal reasons. The TV commercials have to be sought and the ad agencies have to be chased to get the TV ads.

Some ads may be had for the asking and some even without asking but many ads, in fact most ads, are available only by chasing the ad agencies. Here the real test of the national network comes in and it has to keep a well balanced and powerful team in Mumbai for the purpose. Particularly the interests of the DD bulletins have to be borne in mind and the old attitude from AIR that news is to be treated as a stepchild of the organisation has to be discarded.

Some vital changes in the coverage are also called for. There is no doubt that DD news is truthful but the emphasis seems to be on the fact that the news has to guard against the onslaughts of the opposition and the media which are bent upon the government being toppled and replaced by a more monstrous Congress regime. To correct the image, DD in its news coverage goes to the other extreme of correcting the private channels' coverage. If they say that the Gujarat situation is very bad, the DD news says it is fast improving and near normalcy prevails. The truth is that there is normalcy in the whole of Gujarat, unless the ISI and the VHP have other plans up their sleeves and some more disgruntled and idle brains to carry them out are ready.

The outstation correspondents, specially in the state capitals, have to be kept in check as they are relied upon to project an overall point of view. DD has to depend, and more so the staff, on the state government for various things but that does not mean that it has to yield ground in the vital matter of news. That does not weaken our argument that DD gets in the mater of ads a pittance as compared to the meanest TV channel projecting news. The Mumbai staff must be judged by the noticeable improvement in the matter of ads for the various news bulletins and other non-entertainment programmes. Some editors in Delhi have to cure their tendency to imitate the hostile print media.

Promoting a controversy for the sake of controversy seems to be the guiding star of most TV channels. That seems to be the ideal of NDTV and some of its anchors help project an image of hostility personally also as though they have to identify themselves with the news. This happens in critical situations and even in ordinary circumstances. Ordinary circumstances are those when at the end of the bulletin we are presented by the NDTV with something which it considers extraordinary but which happens all the while. It is known by different names, like "sarokar", but serves the same purpose.

Once upon a time, the mode was for success stories from the rural areas and some urban areas too to be projected but the TV agencies pick up stories from anywhere to project their own image that they are presenting the stories picked up from various states with an anti-government bias. They hope to do better that way with the ad agencies which they presume to be anti-government.

The NDTV, linked as it is to the Star foreign channel, tries also to provoke controversies like it did when J. Jayalalithaa was refused nomination by as many as four returning officers for the Tamil Nadu state assembly elections in 2001 April and later the same year when the Supreme Court ruled that she was wrongly sworn in as Chief Minister of Tamil Nadu. The news presentor asked the channel's Chennai correspondent to report immediately if there were demonstrations in favour of Jayalalithaa on the returning officers decision and the Supreme Court's order. This was in line with the Hindi news presenter, who later switched to DD as news presenter for a fairly long time, asking the NDTV's New Delhi correspondent why the seat reserved for the then Punjab Chief Minister at the BJP rally in the capital was vacant in the 1999 Lok Sabha elections. The switch from NDTV to DD comes handy to some TV journalists provided it is lucrative. In fact, the same person acted as Rajiv Gandhi's guide when he was Prime Minister and when she had organised for some women to interview him on DD of course.

The news presenter has a duty to perform but the provocation of the correspondents on the ground seems to indicate the electronic media's approach to create a controversy where there is none. The *a priori* assumption that everything under the sun is bad, to prove one's credentials as a reliable medium for ads, is wrong. Here one has to be careful in choosing targets as the Indian and normal human to blame someone else for one's failure is to be taken into account.

Before we take up the question of filling up time in the early hours of the day, we have to take into consideration that TV channels get away with the impression that it is enough to project different points of view by interviewing people, usually politicians, known to the viewers as representing the particular viewpoint. But they also have a duty to perform when they have to say which of the points is right and which wrong. Or they have to tell the viewers how they would themselves resolve the issue by presenting it in limelight. It is not enough to bring different points of view which is an easy exercise because the temptation to see one's face on the TV is great and that incites people to be interviewed for a news programme. They have to tell the viewers where they themselves stand.

The early part of the day is the time when all news media face the problem of the paucity of fresh news. That is an old newsman's problem because the news as we understand it develops and become a story to be broadcast after about 5 p.m. That is in the nature of newsfall because news is just not available before the time. Sometimes when Parliament is in session Parliament comes to the rescue of the media but it is not in session the year round and nowadays the story would be somewhat identical for all the days the two houses are in session because more often than not the two houses are adjourned for someone like Raghuvans Prasad shouts and the houses are adjourned.

Some find it easy to fill out time by foreign stories but for that to happen the TV channels have to find the visuals to go with the story and often for the channel with a twenty-four hour coverage there is a problem of avoiding too much repetition and there is a danger of the channel losing its well-earned reputation for a balance. It tries to fill out time by interviewing people of some repute as when it got an interview with the Star actor of the Hindi screen Shah Rukh Khan about his new film (now too old) Ashoka which some say flopped by the time he was interviewed by the channel. Nothing of any consequence was said in the interview but it helped the agency in overcoming the problem of lack of stories.

The actor defended loudly the imaginary relaxation of the great Ashoka with his girl friend in his more youthful days before he attacked Kalinga (modern Orissa). You twist history to allow for a sequence of dance and song and the audience which is the real judge of a film's worth because it pays to see the film has no option but like it. It said that no Indian film maker has ventured to make a film on Gandhiji because of their must for a dance and song sequence (and his autobiography would provide encugh justification for several dance and song sequences) but the audience would permit it. Mahatma, when he is material enough for a historical on him, would perhaps allow for a series of dances as Shah Rukh Khan did with Ashoka but it is likely that audience tastes would be more refined. That, of course, is a matter of hope, some say it is a forlon hope. At present Bollywood is engaged in imitating Hollywood and churning out many a violent film.

In any case, the agency got an interview with the actor who in turn got free publicity for his film. Is it too much to hope that Bollywood would attempt a film without the dance and song sequence and it would produce a worthwhile film on Gandhiji without a single song as did Richard Attenborough for his film Gandhi for which he won many accolades and even now the echoes can be heard, like the knighthood for the main actor who played the part of the Mahatma. Surprisingly no question of this type was put to Shah Rukh Khan in the interview.

Of the other channels enough has been said about their general approach and about some, of their particular attitude. From a vocal and vociferous supporter of the BJP, the Jain TV has become a champion of the Congress Party. The Zee TV news has acquired the status of a balanced projector of news and views and tries hard, subject to the remarks made earlier about TV channels in general. As stated earlier, the NDTV, aligned to the Star foreign satellite TV, is in many ways the electronic counterpart of the print media giant, *The Times of India*. It believes that too much is bad in India and it needs to be brought before the public, although unlike the *Indian Express* which referred to India as a "disaster" country, refrains from saying it. One need not be misled by the large number of its viewers on occasion because thats a media gimmick. It is indeed a surprise that the boss of NDTV, Pranay (who spells his name with a double 'n') Roy manages to project himself as CII (Confederation of Indian Industries) man allows all the anti-Indian stuff in his news bulletins.

What the people want to see in the news and what the credibility of the media is, is a difficult question but when the bulletins are packed with ulterior material which is not news and therefore, newsworthy, it shows a motive. And it is a moot question when the TV channels project day in and day out sensational stuff what the clear motive of the electronic media is. The conclusion is inescapable that sensation is the soul of news which must be highlighted as the most essential element.

The Taliban regime may have let down some media in India by quickly falling to the American and Northern Alliance pressure and collapsed like a house of cards and only some pockets resisted the onslaught when the select media expected the regime to fight back. The media, of the print variety and the electronic type, had to eat humble pie and bite the dust but the regime collapsed and the media joined the more sensible elements in lambasting the Taliban. *The Times of India,* which lost nobody in the US-Afghan war because it sent out nobody from its vast array of correspondents to cover the fighting (it did so much for the Taliban and Al-Qaida from its base) had the common trait with the NDTV which also covered the war sitting in New Delhi (as its name signifies).

The people realised that there was no use crying over spilt milk when they saw the Tajiks, Uzbeks and Pashtuns fight the Talibans (who are mostly Pashtuns). Some of the Indian media tried to project Osama bin Laden as some kind of a hero when he was around and being worshipped by some Muslims.

The sports channels, mainly Star Sports and ESPN,

who actually were rivals but later came together as Star-ESPN, are watched by many in this country. The DD Sports for the past few years has been playing a useful role but it is not clear as it goes completely haywire when it covers an international event like the India-England or India-Zimbabwe series. Having bid for the television rights and having been chosen by the BCCI for it, it is not clear why the channel chose to sell out to a group of TV broadcasters including Australian TV channel who control the channel and call the shots.

So much so, that when England was playing, a team of English commentators took over and Indian, were reduced to a secondary role. Similar was the case when Zimbabwe was playing and we found that a two some, Robin Jackman and Chris Cowdry, had complete control of the medium. No doubt they displayed a good report with the Indians some of whom are called to comment on Australia-South Africa series in South Africa. Ravi Shastri is the Indian commentator who comments on the tests as well as the one-dayers. Why this discrimination against Indians in their own home? The English commentators were so overbearing—particularly Ian Botham who was all for England—so that the Indians felt out of place. No doubt the Englishmen were all former test players of eminence and renowned for their cricketing prowess but surely the English media would not tolerate the Indians being treated like the Indians were in their homes. England resorted to negative tactics in the second test which it continued in the third and final test but while the English press played the tactics, the TV commentary was silent except for a former England captain, Bob Willis who was an exception to the rule.

Similarly against Zimbabwe, Robin Jackman

aggressively campaigned for its victory in the test series and the one-dayers. Chris Cowdry was a passive supporter of Jackman but on crucial occasions he came to the aid of the visitora. Robin Jackman is a familiar figure to the Indian viewers but now he took up cudgels for Zimbabwe aggressively and his usual placid self was considerably disfigured during the Indo-Zimbabwe series. As usual, he and Cowdry were both appreciative of the many points in favour of individual Indians but they were so intent on Zimbabwe winning at least the one-day series in India that their disappointment was evident.

DD Sports does a commendable job covering many of the important sports events including Indian international events as described above. Sometimes for lack of fresh material including visuals, we have to suffer coverage of the Sydney Olympic games which were staged quite some time ago. To offer competition to the two sports channels it will have to do considerably more. The channels, ESPN and Star Sports, have become Indian in many respects and even cover Indian domestic events. This is in addition to covering international cricket from New Zealand, South Africa, West Indies and Australia.

That, however, does not prevent two daily bulletins, Star Sports sportsline and ESPN Sportcentre, from going at times all out against India and generally also critical about India and its cricketer, Sachin Tendulkar, and unjustifiably attacking in its approach. The channels exploit Indian sentiments fully and use Sachin's image in their promos but that is no guarantee against India not being attacked. It seems their editors are somewhat fed up with the projection of Sachin and want to have it out in this manner in their bulletins. The editors utilised fully the anti-Indian stuff being written in the print media some of whom can be known by readers of this book. The editors proudly recount the "exploits" of Englishmen who are supposed to have beaten West Indians and Pakistanis.

The two channels have their own ratings which nobody has recognised or quoted which would be proof of their acceptance. For no reason, Pakistan which got beaten by practically everyone always go up in the estimate of the channel raters and manages to go up and up.

Does the watching of TV channels make the morning newspaper redundant? This is a moot question and for that we have to examine some more evidence. First of all, the circulation of the leading dailies and the circulation of the press as a whole has not gone down[1]. The Press in India is an authentic compilation of the Registrar of Newspapers in India (RNI) and it has not shown a decline in the circulation of the press as a whole. If anything, the total circulation goes up from year to year. Even the circulation of the Hindi and other Indian languages has far outstripped that of the English newspapers although the English newspapers influence the press in general otherwise.

But it is a fact that the busy urban reader hardly gets time to study in detail the news so carefully presented by many a newspaper. In other words, he has hardly the time to read "between the lines" and any time at all to read the news in detail. He as to get ready for his office in the morning and has little time except to look at the headlines and the sports page or pages. He has no time to study the paper on the way or in office and in the evening when he returns home he finds relaxation in watching TV and while he surfs the channels he eyes the TV news channels.

He thus gets into the habit of watching Aaj Tak or some other channel of his liking. The newspapers know his habits and therefore prefer to pack all they have to say in their headlines which are sometimes deceptive in the extreme. The average reader finds in the headlines an answer to his problems but the newspapers do not know that he derives much knowledge by surfing channels. When he finds in the morning that the papers broadly conform to the late evening newscast and confirm what they have been saying, the question arises in his mind: are the morning papers redundant?

The print media have, of course, other uses. Before we go into it, let us take note of the fact that with the advent of TV the social habits are also undergoing a major change. Guests who have a habit of dropping in without previous notice are generally not welcome and many of them are also watching prime time TV when the households are on to their favourite programmes and the entire family is watching TV. While many families are still considering buying the morning paper, the possession of a TV set is a must for them. Whether the family is middle class or lower middle class they must have their TV. For the upper classes, who watch TV after attending a cocktail party in the evening, there is no question of the kind. They have both, the daily newspaper and the TV set. For families which cannot afford a set, the possession of a set is something which has high priority, in fact the highest.

The result is that people in the hutment cluster will forego a meal but if they can they will go in for a TV set and otherwise there is the neighbour and the employer of a help maid. The print media are there for record. If you have a newspaper you can refer to a certain event and get its details which you cannot from the TV programme. Assuming that the newspaper has published the story (a big if in certain cases), you can study or just pursue the relevant details of foreign dignitary's speech at the banquet given in his honour by the President or Prime Minister or something of the like. The list of what you need to consult or refer to, even if you are not a professional journalist or a researcher, can be widened to include the current affairs, sports or business.

For you to get it from your favourite TV programme you have to have special equipment and unless you deploy it at the time of the telecast, the effort goes waste.

Some difficulties can also be encountered in respect of the print media but they are less insurmountable. A newspaper may be sold in "raddi" for its resale value or may be used by the wife as fuel or aid to fuel. Those contingencies are, of course there, but a little forethought on the user's part would, obviate the difficulty but the same cannot be said for your TV set. We have referred to the cosy give and take between a newspaper and the TV station. In major cities this is possible and when the TV develops a local medium this will become more prevalent. But already there is enough give and take between newspapers and the electronic medium.

The question remains whether TV news channel watching makes the buying of the daily newspaper redundant. The problem of curious member of the household wanting to watch his news programme while the rest of the family sees with some expectation its favourite serial is an old one which has affected radio listening or faced by radio listeners in the past when radio dominated the media scene. Newspapers can take comfort from the fact that they survived the competition from the powerful Radio medium and they can hope to survive the TV medium competition, although that is going to be rather difficult.

For the present, to answer a question like the watching TV, particularly the news channels, would make the buying of your daily redundant would need more inputs like research into habits and the factors which influence families to watch TV and buy a newspaper.

An interesting report appeared in *The Hindustan Times*, Delhi, to the effect that the Star TV network is acquiring equity in the highly successful *Aaj Tak* news channel along with vehement contradiction from the horses mouth[2]. We have referred to the high degree of proficiency of the Aaj Tak channel and its phenomenal success in winning the confidence of the viewers and consequently advertisers and have remarked that it would appear that news appears to flow with ads which are more than we can stomach. The report quoting figures confirms all that.

Launched on December 31, 2000, when it broke the umbilical cord with DD Metro channel, which, for some reasons, it does not like to be reminded of, the news channel was a financial success within just six months. We should think that such a large body of viewership which accounted for its financial viability was mainly due to its sticking to the narrow path of truth, not sensation, although its editors find it attractive at times to indulge in sensation.

The Hindustan Times quoted the channel's CEO to say that the Star story was without any foundation. The paper adds that the *Aaj Tak's* viewership exceeds that of all the other news channels put together. In concrete terms, its share comes a poor second with only a 22 per cent. The New Delhi TV, which is bilingual but still linked with the foreign channel that Star is third with 17 per cent. The totally foreign channels like BBC has just 3 per cent and CNN and its American rival NBC have two per cent each.

The success of the *Aaj Tak* channel in cornering the glory and its phenomenal economic success is ascribed by the report to the channel's "single minded" approach to news. Whereas the other channels boast of their analysis and discussions the report says the *Aaj Tak* focus is on news. This is not entirely true. As for discussions, the channel invites known or what it described as experts for a discussion in its 10 p.m. newscast. This practice is followed almost on all occasions when the need for a panel discussion arises, or even otherwise. The need for analysis does not seem to arise because the editors of the channel themselves internally sum up the situation, otherwise left hanging by just presenting two sides of the coin, or they think so, in the other channels.

The success of the channel is mainly due to treating news not as a commodity but as a sacred trust and to be handled with care and with more than an eye on credibility. Some changes in the format are always necessary and they are incorporated from time to time. When the need is felt at the organisational or editorial level. What *The Hindustan Times* reporter speculates could be the real reason for the Star float that they "think" of acquiring the equity of *Aaj Tak*. There is some talk as the NDTV has, as alleged, told the Star network that they would cut off links with the Star network and Star may launch its own news channel in Hindi. The network thinks it would hit two birds with one stone. The NDTV loss would be obviated and the network would get a share of ad revenue.

But it is not easy to establish the credibility of the channel and hope to get a share of the ad revenue. Once, of course, the viewers turn to it the ad revenue automatically follows because the advertisers want to cash in on the success of the enterprise. But they first want to be sure that there is an audience. At this rate, DD bulletins have a captive audience and a number of viewers choose to listen in to the DD bulletins but it is not the first choice of the admen. In other words, they have to be chased and perhaps the message has gone home to DD.

There are other factors which have to be taken into consideration. There is, for example, the factor favourable to *Aaj Tak* that it is uplinked from Delhi itself whereas its rivals have to depend on Hong Kong for it. The *Aaj Tak* team went into Afghanistan proper during the war which, more than you can say even of the *Times of India,* the richest Indian paper whose correspondent, Siddharath Varadarajan is now touring Pakistan and earlier visited Afghanistan but was nowhere near during the fighting. The paper was not represented at all in the war. It did not avail of the facilities when Madhavrao Scindia, the Congress leader died on his way to Kanpur in an aircrash. The correspondents of *The Hindustan Times* and of the TV channel, *Aaj Tak,* died with him, because they were on the same plane with him and availed of the offer to cover his party rally.

The *Aaj Tak* did not have the advantage of Zee News which was the first TV news channel to branch out on their own and had the advantage to enter as the new venture of news. Until then *Aaj Tak* had gone with the DD Metro which added to mutual strength.

Meanwhile, a report appeared in the *Business Times* columns of *Times of India*[3] saying Raveena Raj Kohli is to head the Star news channel. This meant that NDTV, whose contract with the Star foreign channel is ending in April 2003, will set up separate shop and may ask that like *Aaj Tak* it be allowed to uplink from Delhi itself instead of Hong Kong from where the Star is uplinked at present. Kohli earlier headed the Nine Gold on DD Metro which ended in disaster in 2001 after successfully running for a year and solved many of DD's financial woes. The contract came apart when Nine Gold demanded better terms for renewing the DD association, Kohli is said to have no experience of News work but in the parlance of the TV that matters little.

References

1. Author's book, *Indian Press Since 1955*, Publications Division, Delhi, may be pursued for the purpose.
2. *The Hindustan Times*, Delhi, March 31, 2002.
3. "Star India reshapes top management " *The Times of India*, Delhi, April 12, 2002.

Seven

Sports under Pressure

In the media's view all is grist to the mill, even sports. It comes handy to the media's desire to present it as sensational when all news subserves the purpose of the game. As awareness is spreading fast and interest in sports advances by leaps and bounds controversy never ceases. In fact, sports abounds in controversies—for every international event there are several conflicts and controversies. There is a perpetual controversy over why Leander Pais and Mahesh Bhupathy cannot get together after they are playing for some time and are recognised as world beaters in doubles tennis. Why they separate—once and twice. No correspondent has ever tried to find out why they cannot get on. There is no dearth of sports correspondents in the media, the print variety and the TV channels which constitute our electronic media.

When Sachin Tendulkar is a great star, almost a god, there is nothing sacred to the media. They rake up the old conflict—Sachin versus Lara although Lara might have tried to put an end to all controversies by praising Sachin. There is a perpetual controversy about Ganguly's captaincy of the test squad in cricket—that he is lazy, that he is arrogant, and so on. If he is lazy how is it that he scores centuries and is able to pick the right man for the job—Dinesh Mongia as opening partner even though he is a left-hand batsman. If Yuvraj scored beautifully in the fourth and fifth one-dayer against Zimbabwe and if he is not picked for the test squad for the West Indies another controversy erupts. It is not realised that the team for the one-dayers against the West Indies is yet to be selected and in all probability Yuvraj will find a place in it.

Controversy is the soul of news and more so, in sports, we are told. This is a situation from which it is difficult to get out because there is no end to it. The controversy goes on and on. Some blithe souls try to get at the roots of the controversy when the sports editor of *The Times of India* tried to delve deep into the BCCI (Board of Cricket Control in India) and even predicted that A.C. Muthiah would be re-elected as the BCCI President. That was on the morning of the vote and he was proved wrong because it was the other candidate, Jagmohan Dalmiya, who was elected. We have referred to it in an earlier chapter.

There are, in fact, more controversies in sports than in politics, the second best in so far as the media are concerned. But the controversy in politics interests the media more. We have seen it but as the interest in sports has increased beyond all expectations the controversy is increasing and one does not know how the whole thing would end at all if it ever will.

Many fallacies persist as the sports correspondents write their copy. *The Hindustan Times* is one of those papers which specialises in this type of writing. Its correspondent reporting on one of the one-dayers writes: "Chasing targets is not India's forte. If anything it is their *bete noire*. Even a modest score becomes colossal for them."[1] The writer forgets what happened in Dhaka when India chased a Pakistan total of 310 (considered a huge one-day score) and achieved the target in the last over and won the match.

There are more glorious instances of "chasing" which

the learned sports writers conveniently ignore or forget. For example, in the Coca Cola Cup in Sharjah in 1998 Sachin Tendulkar scored back-to-back centuries against Australia and first took India into the final of the tournament and then won it for India. The next day he won the final for his country against Australia who had a big score in its innings. That was a memorable performance but there were even greater things to follow. In the series against Zimbabwe in the Hyderabad match in 2002, defeat faced India when Kaif was still batting and he was joined by Yuvraj Singh. Both of them turned the defeat into glorious victory as the paper along with the other media recorded. They were chasing a target. This did not prove "colossal" for the Indians.

This is not written in the spirit of carping criticism but a statement of facts to show that what the correspondent concerned wrote was not a fact. Why do the writers persist in their presumption? It is difficult to say except that it is fashionable nowadays to blame the test or one-day players for everything and give them less than the credit they deserve. Everytime India plays an international event, the sports writers want India to win, irrespective of the calibre of the opposition. They are also interested in winning matches but that does not appear to be the concern of these writers. India must win seems to be the primary concern of the writers.

This concern does not always get translate into the reports of the media. Davis Cup (tennis) offers an example. When Chille played India some years ago, Rio their star player remarked that India could win the doubles match and nothing else. This was highlighted and played up by several media including *The Indian Express* which seems to specialise in sports. Eventually, only Rio won because he is such a good player and India beat Chille 4-1 in the Davis Cup. Playing up the statements made by the visiting team spokesmen, and at times even some members not authorised to speak for the team, becomes a weapon in the armoury of the media which are interested in creating sensation for its own sake. The media are inclined to believe that more sensation means more circulation and the lovers of sports would read or watch that particular paper or TV channel.

Papers like *The Times of India* invite the spokesmen or those known for their views to comment and give interviews to the paper in such cases. That is said to be in the fairness of things because its correspondents are supposed to report from the Indian point of view and the opposition must get its point of view. This is a perfectly valid argument but it also hides the fact that its rival paper, *The Hindustan Times,* has cornered all Indian writers of note and there is nothing left for it. When the opposition champions support the tactics employed against Indian players of note, that amounts to projecting the point of view more prominently than justified. The England captain employed negative tactics against Sachin Tendulkar in the second test between the two countries and the paper carried Botham's defence of the tactics whereas almost the entire English press gave hell to their captain.

There were other voices in favour and in defence of the negative play and its repercussions can be heard even now. When Sunil Gavaskar who is considered a legend in cricket and respected in all cricket playing nations called the English habit of complaining too much as whining and the cricket the English team played as boring there were not too many expressions in defence of the English team but Gavaskar was attacked by a writer in Wisden.

The media are so planned as to project everything

which is relevant or irrelevant concerning the tourists or those visited by India such as West Indies or England. The media are overanxious to project their point of view which is quite understandable but often enough. The goal is overshot with the result that their point of view is more pronounced than the Indian viewpoint. That is done quite deliberately because the media seem to think that if the readers or viewers are scared that will serve the purpose of getting more and more people to be attracted to the media.

Sometimes the particular paper miscalculates the result of a match in progress and lands itself into incalculable disgrace. *The Indian Express* (Ahmedabad edition)[2] is an example in question. It first highlighted the "success" of the Pakistan team, then touring Australia, and the second test was in progress. When the paper found that the Pakistanis were in a winning position it headlined "Wizards of Pak: Aussies down, almost out". The Australians, however, took command the next day when Adam Gilchrist and Justin Langer, both left-handers, who scored centuries scoring freely yet carefully. Gilchrist remained unbeaten on 149 while Langer was out when the target was about to be achieved.

Without any qualm of conscience, the paper said the following day "Wizards of Oz: Justin, Adam win it for hosts." In the nxst column of the story (actually a double column) *The Express* headlined "Pak mourn turn of wheel, defeat".

Few examples of quick-change can be seen or recalled. Nobody expected the paper to jump to a conclusion so suddenly, knowing the state of the game and the Australian grit not to face defeat except under unavoidable circumstances. Obviously the paper was delighted when the Pakistanis were winning but it move a sudden transformation. Apparently, it had more faith than justified in the Pakistani bowlers and less in the Australian batsmen although Gilchrist and Langer are known to turn the tables.

The papers enjoy more freedom in sports page than others and the fancy writing of features as news abounds in reporting the sports stories. Only the headings come to the readers' rescue because they have normally to reveal the result. Reporting the outcome of the Indo-New Zealand tie in Guwahati in November 1999 we had the experience when the headline informed us of the outcome "Cairns helps Kiwis level series". (We quoted earlier from the paper). The point made here is that the print media ignores the same advice that news must be written as news and not as feature. What if the deskman also takes it into his head and gives a fanciful heading without the result.

The papers observe no rules when it comes to reporting or writing sports stories and there is a kind of free for all prevailing. The headlines also at times hide more than they reveal. *The Hindustan Times* on April 3, 2002, headlined "Pressure on Windies" which is a case in point. You can make any meaning out of the heading. *The Times of India,* on the same day, "NZ Chances brighten in dim light" playing upon "bright" and "dim". *The Hindustan Times* was more explicit on the subject when it said "Astle gives Kiwis victory chance" although it must be admitted that Nathan Astle being an all-rounder, one may look to the bowling column rather than the batting scores. *The Times* had a heading "After pride, the pockets take a hit" which could mean anything to sports lovers heading was about a proposal of the South African board for cricket for a cut in the salaries of the players who fail to live up to expectations and perform poorly. Where does pride find a place in all this thing?

For the readers who invariably refer to the sports pages before they leave for the office there is a mixed bag when the only explicit heading "Ganguly leaves for West Indies" which leaves little to imagination is a kind of exception. When the Indian coach, John Wright, said two different things for two newspapers, it would appear so because the headlines for the story differ. *The Times* headline is : "Changing nature of wickets will suit India, says Wright" while the heading in the *HT* was "Slow wickets will aid India, says Wright" on the same day April 3, 2002, he said the West Indies wickets had gone slower over the years and this should help the Indian bowlers. *The Times* deskman, under instructions from the bosses that they must say something different from others in their headings made him change the "slower" into "changing" nature of pitches.

England which made big noise about its performance in India and got beaten in the test series, 1-0, lost the last test in New Zealand, which country they visited immediately after the hosts drew the test series by beating England in the third test. Captain Nasser Hussain said in New Zealand at the end of the test and one-dayer series that he was no whinging captain. (Memories of the Indian tour). Meeting the press after the defeat in the third test at Auckland' Eden Park Hussain New Zealand Captain, of Indian descent, said. "The last thing I want to do is sit here and be like a whinging England captain."[3]

The defeat was so emphatic and the New Zealand bowlers were so effective with their medium to medium fast stuff that with the first three days lost to weather, with only 82 overs bowled as against 270 maximum admissible, the New Zealand team had to wage battle on the fourth and fifth day when the rain held and bad light was overcome with the help of electric lights. The New Zealand batsmen refused the bad lights offered by umpires (India's S. Venkataraghavan was there).

The England captain, in using the phrase "whinging" was using a Gavaskar charge against the England tourist team. They were always complaining against one thing or another. First some English players would not come because they were too afraid of the US-Afghan war spreading to India and finally when they came complained against one thing or another. *The Times of India,* which did not carry Hussain's "no whinging captain" comment was one of the important media to boost their morale after their defeat in the first test at Mohali. By subtle use of its media power and other means, including the use of its columns by Ian Botham, one of the all-time greats of English cricket who seemed to travel all over with the English team—Sri Lanka, Pakistan and Zimbabwe in the earlier tour and India and New Zealand in the recently concluded tour end seemed to have arrangements to capture the commentators' microphone on TV channels over the countries, the paper went all out to help the England tourists.

The media's ways are sometimes inscrutable. They appear so at times but they can be deciphered all the same. The main motivation of the media is the Indians in all sports must win and at the same time they seek to highlight the achievements, real or believed, of the opposition. Anything is grist to the media mill and some controversy or the other is floated from time to time to keep the pot boiling and sometimes this is really important. Thus, Kapil Dev, another legend in cricket, may say the media must not be too prying and himself keep off the media for a time when he is the subject of charges in the match fixing controversy, but once in the clear he ventured forth and accused great names of lack of commitment.

Both Sachin Tendulkar and Sourav Ganguly, the Indian cricket captain, played it rather coolly when Kapil Dev floated the controversy but the media tried to take advantage of it. They, however, did not succeed in their efforts. The media tried their hand at another aspect of it but there also they failed. Rather out of frustration they came back to the selection process in two games where the media are welcomed with open arms. We are referring to cricket and hockey where the selection committee or the organisers are open to arguments and willingly or otherwise welcome the media's intrusion. Why these two games are chosen it will be difficult to say because other games are more or less equally popular judging by the popular interest evinced in their stars performance.

For example, tennis because of India's success in the Davis Cup matches has become quite popular. Similarly, the success of Pulela Gopichand in the All-England competition and subsequent Japan open where he reached the semi-final stage and then lost has caught the attention of the media. But no interest whatsoever is displayed at the selection stage. Why this apathy?

The well laid out procedure of the appointment of a selection committee in the game of cricket opens the way for the media which also knows of the tremendous public interest in the game to take interest in the selection. But typically the media practise by now the well known formula "sensation, not truth". If the selectors choose X and not Y they ask questions and indulge in criticism, knowing the selectors' compulsions. They are damned if they do, they are damned if they don't. In the process, they play their favourites. The same goes for hockey.

References

1. *The Hindustan Times*, Delhi, Nov. 15,1999.
2. *Indian Express*, Ahmedabad, Nov. 22 and 23, 1999.
3. *The Hindustan Times*, Delhi April 4, 2002.

Eight

Media Freedom

We have mentioned more than once the freedom from any interference of the governmental machinery in the working of the media ever since the Vajpayee regime came to power in March 1998. The media enjoyed the freedom even under the UF government in 1996-97 and the total freedom the two sets of media, the print media and the electronic media, by which is meant the satellite TV channels (because the important medium of radio is at present a national monopoly) are enjoying is not very long in terms of time.

True, the first move in the direction of freeing the media was made when L.K. Advani was I and B Minister in the Morarji Desai government when he appointed a committee under B.G. Verghese (journalist of eminence), to frame recommendations for freeing the government media of AIR and Doordarshan. At that time, the radio mattered most and DD came late when the national programme of DD was introduced, when the DD centres at Delhi, Bombay (since named Mumbai) and Chennai were linked. But it really became an effective weapon in the armoury of the media when satellite TV became operational to coincide with the Iraq war of the United States (functioning under a UN resolution) in 1991.

By that time the Congress Party was back in power and the subtle and open interference of the government machinery began to make its appearance. The oppressive rules of the Congress Party ended with the elections of May 1996 which were contested in an atmosphere of freedom. The B.G. Verghese committee recommended more or less complete freedom for the two important media but before a bill incorporating the recommendations could be passed the Morarji Desai government fell and soon after that the Congress Party returned to power. The return to power of Indira Gandhi was marked by the rise of terrorism in Punjab and under her son Rajiv Gandhi's rule as Prime Minister, it spread to Jammu and Kashmir. It became a reality to reckon with, under the one-year rule of the V.P. Singh government, when Rajiv Gandhi led an official delegation (although he was no longer Prime Minister and held no official position except that of the leader of opposition). We are mentioning all this because Rajiv Gandhi it was, who caused the maximum harm to Indian polity by raising all manner of questions during the Srinagar visit and the AIR and DD covered him fully as though he was still Prime Minister.

A curious thing happened on the day Rajiv Gandhi succeeded his mother after her assassination. He was on his way to Delhi from Calcutta and held no official position except that of an MP (Rajiv Gandhi was General Secretary of the AICC at that time). But as Congress affairs went it was almost certain that he was to be sworn in as the Prime Minister. But how was he to know that the mother, who was the Prime Minister, had died? The media highlighted the news that Rajiv Gandhi listened to the BBC for confirmation of what he heard from various unconfirmed reports.

What happened was a curious thing exposing many weaknesses in the Congress government. AIR was ordered not to broadcast anything except that the Prime Minister had been shot by her Sikh security guards and she had been removed to the All India Institute of Medical Sciences (AIIMS). This was the version which was broadcast from hour to hour in AIR's hourly bulletins and a little longer version in the longer bulletins like 2 p.m. and 6 p.m.

What can AIR do in the circumstances? I was out but had a fair knowledge of what was going on. The organisation was capable of a balanced presentation, of how the PM was shot at, how Sonia Gandhi removed her to hospital and possibly R.K. Dhawan, her special assistant whom Sonia did not like a bit accompanied her to the AIIMS, how Rajiv Gandhi was expected in Delhi as the mother had few chances of survival. The print media made a play of fact that AIR was incompetent and Rajiv Gandhi had to listen to the BBC for the news of his mother's likely death without knowing anything at all. Rajiv Gandhi who was all in all even while Indira groomed him for the position of the Prime Minister did nothing about freeing AIR from official control, neither in his unofficial capacity or later as Prime Minister.

AIR was a handy tool in the hands of the Congress rulers and once the Congress comes back to power there is no end to Sonia's day dreaming and the media are aiding her in her venture to become the Prime Minister somehow the conditions can be imagined. The Prasar Bharati Act is there for all to see and without any compunction the Minister of Information and Broadcasting, who was a small officer in the railways who cashed in on N.T. Rama Rao's name as PUC Chowdhary and later switched on to the Congress Party and later got elected to the 12th Lok Sabha for one term and later got defeated on that party ticket used the act to his own advantage. He was loyalist then an NTR. He could be nominated in the elections to the 14th Lok

Sabha or brought to the house in a by-election provided the voters of Andhra Pradesh were to turn against their Chief Minister, N. Chandra Babu Naidu. There is in any cases no dearth of deputies of Sonia who could "effectively" handle the I and B portfolio.

There is no doubt that the Congress Party will wield the big stick at the media (and some subtle methods too) if and when it comes to power at the Centre. That remains a big "if", much bigger than some people may think, but if ever the Congress Party returns to power the media have had it. All the freedom that the media now enjoy would disappear in a whiff in the thin air and the *danda* (stick) would be back. Many of the states would have to fall in line and so also the print media and the TV channels. The CPIM General Secretary, Harkishan Singh Surjeet who made in early 1999 and even later in the elections to the 13th Lok Sabha, his one point programme to put Sonia on the throne of Delhi but failed is at the game again. The media without realising the consequences are backing the Congress leader and Surjeet to the hilt.

Much as they would regret and hold rallies, (remember the mile-long media procession against Rajiv Gandhi's defamation bill in 1988-89?) that would be like regretting at leisure. Remember the case of Shaheen Sehbai, the editor of the biggest Pakistani newspaper, the News, and *The Times of India* highlighting his plight by publishing an interview with him carefully editing portions which would offend ISI (what connection the paper has with the most diabolical agency?). No Indian editor has the guts to act as Sehbai did and no paper would be prepared to suffer the loss as the *News* and *Jung* boss was not prepared to do. If he was fully exposed, no Indian boss would be prepared to suffer a loss in revenue.

I recall the case of the Commerce and Industry Minister T.T. Krishnamachari and the *Statesman* reporter, Hansraj Vohra. Both of them are dead but as I was involved with the case and as the matter has some relevance to the Sehbai case., I make no apologies for recounting it here. TTK, as the minister was known, was appointed by Nehru in 1957 as additional minister of the newly created Iron and Steel Ministry. Vohra who was covering the ministries of Coal and Iron and Steel also covered for his paper, the *Statesman* of Calcutta and Delhi, the Planning Commission. He had been handed a paper on the Durgapur project, the third steel plant in the public sector after Rourkela and Bhilai. At that time the Durgapur was still a project and the late K.C. Neogi, who was a member of the Planning Commission and a former minister, had prepared a paper objecting to the materialisation of Durgapur. Neogi was from Bengal and like today's ministers he thought first of his state and of the country later, he would not have put his name to the paper.

Vohra had been handed that paper and based on it without revealing Neogi's name and his status, he wrote a story, saying the Durgapur project had not reached a state of finality. TTK asked me to put out a denial, simple and straightforward, to his story which I did. I did not know of the Neogi's paper at that time nor the person who had given that paper till *The Statesman* correspondent told me about it. I told Vohra not to bother about the denial but let the desk handle it. He did not listen to my advice and made a front page story of my simple contradiction. Apparently he was concerned about his credibility and the paper's credibility. The Statesman those days was still owned and edited by the British.

TTK was furious at Vohra's second story. He

immediately ordered stoppage of all advertisement from the C and I ministry and his new ministry of Iron and Steel and release of all material to the paper from Calcutta where the C and I had a big set-up.

The PIO, acting as a spokesman of the I and B ministry tried to intervene and accompanied me to the Minister but to no avail. Within a week, however the British-edited *Statesman* apologised to the minister in its editorial in its own way and his own secretaries intervening. Normalcy was restored in the relations between Vohra and TTK's two ministries. Vohra was, however, not satisfied with the situation and moved later to *The Times of India* which posted him in the US as their Washington correspondent where I met him.

The British-edited and owned *Statesman* could not bear the loss of ad revenue and the consequent blacklisting of the paper by TTK, a powerful Minister in the Nehru government, and most proprietors would yield before the authorities as the proprietor of the Pakistani newspapers had yielded and cowtowed before the Pakistani authorities which itself was acting as the darling agency, the ISI, who had ordered the PIO in Pakistan to call the editor and when the editor did not yield immediately called the boss who was relaxing somewhere in England. The Pakistani bureaucracy does not believe in half measures and goes all the way when the ISI is involved and orders the media to act.

We deliberately said most Indian proprietors would gladly carry out the orders of the government. We have Indira Gandhi's unpopular emergency as a guide when *The Times of India* was the first paper to go under the censorship regime and *The Indian Express* virtually the last. In fact, it was in force, (the emergency lasted from June 25,

1975 until it was partially lifted on January 19, 1977 and finally removed from the statute book on March 20, 1977).

But alas, the old man R.N. Goenka, the boss of the paper, is no longer alive and the proprietors are split. The editor of the paper breathes in the air of freedom and is considered capable to make his way in the present set-up which is no big deal because under the Vajpayee dispensation there is complete freedom and the media have nothing to fear. Once, however, the Congress rule is back, there will be some twisting and more and more interference of various kinds. Would he then stand up and be counted as an upholder of media freedom and would the bosses stand up? I have grave doubts. In fact, the chain may snap in more senses than one. The same may be the case with other bosses, or the proprietors. It is futile to expect them to stand up for the media and the freedom of the media.

So, even it may not be necessary to bring in a regime of emergency and the PIO's telephone call at midnight might suffice. There may be some misunderstanding but this is inevitable and the same official may not be there all the time. After all, under Indira Gandhi's emergency the old PIO was replaced by a stroke of pen and he was happy that his salary was protected, even when he was made to step down from his PIO ship.

What is the media freedom worth if it is so brittle and could be circumvented by a telephone call of the PIO? Sonia, with her emphasis on minority rights, is not much concerned about the freedom of the media. The stress on the rights of the minorities has obviously much to do about the vote bank politics. It would suit the Congress Party if Sonia keeps on harping on the rights of the minorities to the neglect of media freedom.

We have seen how the media turn their deaf ear to the advice of the Vice President and the Prime Minister who warned the media of the dangers inherent in their approach. In particular, Vajpayee had suggested a self-monitoring device but although the media reported it and gave the Prime Minister's views on the prominence they deserved they treated it as one of those things to be forgotten at leisure, which serve as fillers for the day. In any case, the approach was no more one of concern to the media. In this connection, the media did not even give the report of Home Minister L.K. Advani addressing a conference of journalists at Tirupati (Andhra Pradesh) half the prominence it deserved. Advani went to the Tirupati conference of the national executive of the Journalists Union and advised, journalists to be more responsible because he found them as acting in an irresponsible manner while reporting the incidents of violence in Gujarat.[1] The media rightly played up the incident in Ahmedabad Harijan Ashram of Gandhiji the same day (in next day's papers) and the action taken by the state government in the following day's papers, but the question remains as to why Medha Patkar was at all there at the Ashram of Gandhiji in Ahmedabad. She is *bete noire* to the people of Gujarat and whichever political party sponsored her will have hell to pay.

In his address to the Tirupati session of the newly formed body of journalists Advani said they should care for their credibility and while discharging their functions they should display not only credibility but their professional integrity. He rendered the same advice to journalists "not to *sensationalise*" any issuc. (Emphasis added). Comparing the September 11 attack on the World Trade Centre in New York and the December 13 attack on the Indian Parliament in New Delhi, found fault with the Indian Press finding holes in the NDA government and not appreciating the bravery of the security forces who effectively countered the attack.

There is no doubt that the security forces answered the challenge of the terrorists aptly and defeated their purpose of finishing off the entire political leadership in one stroke. That was the real objective of the attack which was foiled and the terrorists at once failed to achieve their object. It was typical of the media that they failed the nation once more when they treated the event as one more of these terrorist attacks. They considered it as a law and order problem and looked at it from the standpoint of the attack of the terrorists and treated it as an event of concern but that is all.

Atal Bihari Vajpayee was in Singapore during April 2002 where he met a highly interesting personality, Lee Kaun Yew, the founder of modern Singapore and in many respects its architect. He occupied the same office for 30 years in Singapore's City Hall which houses some of the important government offices including the Foreign Office. He ruled Singapore with an iron hand and the determination of an iron leader. Rightly most people in India regard Sardar Patel as the Iron Man of India. In a different sense Lee should be rightly called Singapore's Iron Man.

For the initial period he presided over the British relinquishing their tight control over the eastern empire and later its liquidation. Then he tried to join the newly emerging Malaysia but not finding the new nation to his taste and certainly not the Tungku (Tungku Abdur Rahman, the founder and the first Prime Minister of Malaysia) he got out and founded the newly independent Singapore, a republic in its own rights.

Lee held elections to the National Assembly but ensured that his party, the People's action Party, PAP, secured a comfortable majority and most of its candidates were elected unopposed. Singapore has a unique housing programme which means that in the housing schemes live its citizens, not merely its government servants as they do in India. It takes special care of its citizens, Chinese who are about 75 per cent, Malays, the indigenous people who are about 15 per cent, and Indians who are citizens and are about 8 per cent. The biggest characteristic of the Chinese people is their discipline and hard work. The Malays are easy going but have to work hard in Singapore and the Indians find if they educate their children they occupy high positions in the Singapore government and also know and practise the virtue of hard work and discipline.

There is no scope for freedom as we know it in India. We have the democratic freedom and we have the world's highest media freedom. We have the freedom to choose our elected representatives and the result is that the biggest Assembly, the Uttar Pradesh Assembly, is a hung house, some parties openly canvassing support from the minorities. They say that its main support is based on the formula MY, where M stands for Muslims and Y the castemen of the leader of the Samajwadi party its President, Mulayam Singh Yadav. In an election in which the castemen elect other castemen and Muslims act as vote bank what democracy can you expect if Indian democracy is exposed in the process.

Singapore looks after its citizens and guards its frontiers well so that the surplus population of Malaysia and Indonesia and remote India do not enter its soil. It is strict in implementation of its laws. I was in Singapore as a resident whom it enforced the rule against littering. Within weeks of first announcement the rule was enforced successfully and it attracts European and Japanese tourists to just see its streets clean and no litter thrown on them by careless citizens. The media are well controlled and obey the laws and rules implicitly. The journalists who disobey and write in outside papers (nobody can write against the government in Singapore) are brainwashed and made to confess on the TV that they acted on outside instructions. Not like the Indian media who indulge in the most carping criticism and attack the government and the ruling party while they act as mere figureheads of the opposition parties. Reformed' journalists are taken care of by making them useful members of the Singapore society.

Indians are amazed to see the progress of Singapore as are many other observers. Foreign journalists prefer to stay in Singapore and criticise the neighbouring countries at leisure because they cannot live in Singapore if they attack its leaders and government. Its citizens are well looked after and apparently they do not mind the comparative lack of freedom to express themselves. In a way, Singapore has imbibed the Chinese virtues of discipline and hard work and guided democracy. After all, the Chinese are the most numerous of its citizens—75 per cent or thereabout.

The Chinese in China have a Communist society but are imbued with the racial characteristics, all the same. They are concerned about their bread and butter questions and do not mind the denial of freedom. The Singapore Chinese always look to China although it must be said that Lee Kuan Yew looked to Nehru in his earlier days and the government is more concerned with the welfare of all its citizens, irrespective of their racial origin.

Could we see in India a regime somewhat similar to Singapore's? For that we have to ask whether we can see a regime similar to China's, minus the Communist ideology which is not at all relevant to China as we saw the ethnic element predominate in China and wherever the Chinese live. Singapore is somewhat different but it is essentially racial in all that it has got and does. The Pakistanis make a mess of democracy every time a military ruler steps down or is made to step down after seizing power. After a gap of a few years, the army again takes over and the same exercise is gone over/under a new ruler but essentially nothing changes as the players may change but they play the same game and use the tools.

The racial thinking in Singapore is the same as China. The regime that they have ordained for them bears resemblance to the one found in China. The Chinese care two hoots for freedom of thought. Similarly the Singapore government cares little for such fancy ideas which are greatly valued in India. In India unlimited freedom for the media exists whether there is chaos or conflict in the country. The media must have their freedom to attack the government of the day no matter, under what circumstances the government itself has been made to function when the electorate has failed to give a clear-out verdict.

Instead of admiring Vajpayee for running a coalition under trying circumstances, for half the term of the 13th Lok Sabha, they revel in attacks and criticisms, always toeing the opposition line. This line is not endorsed always by their "valued" readers who vote often against the line followed by the media concerned. They think that the public mood is also along the lines they follow, not realising that soon after the Delhi elections when the Congress Party captured power in the state assembly of Delhi the

BJP swept all the seven seats of the capital in the Lok Sabha elections. That happened in Rajasthan and Madhya Pradesh where also the Congress Party was victorious in the assembly polls. The media in Gujarat however, must have their freedom to attack Narendra Modi and the NDA at the Centre.

We do not know the price we pay for the freedom of the media but it must be heavy and all that for the enrichment of Birla or Jain and, of course, for the sake of a few misguided and prejudiced journalists. It is a moot question how long this situation should be endured by the people. Singapore has achieved efficiency at the cost, we may say, of freedom and whether that freedom should have to be sacrificed always. Singapore is a compact society and for that reason it has sealed off its borders and illegal immigration has almost been wiped out. Once freedom of voting and of the media is allowed there would be ethnic conflicts over why some immigration, legal or illegal, should not be permitted and there would be talk of discrimination against some ethnic group or the other.

As stated before, the advantages of Singapore are many but it has disadvantages too because of its small size and its small population. By clever arrangements like ASEAN the danger of small size and population has been averted and its policy of good relations with India and other countries also helps in standing alone in a complex world. That is as far as good foreign policy can help in preserving national integrity. Arrogance is another thing the Singapore leaders have to guard against.

In the early seventies and late sixties Singapore was worried by the British decision to close down their base in the island. It was worried about the security aspect as well as the employment of thousands of its citizens, mostly of

Indian origin. So the fallout feared was not only from the viewpoint of security but also economic. This fear voiced by Lee who was Prime Minister then soon after the elections to the National Assembly which the ruling party, the PAP, had as usual won hands down. However, the fears were proved unfounded, mainly for two reasons both interlinked. First, the surplus employees of the British base were all absorbed in the expansion of the economy of Singapore (and some Indians returning to India in expectation of comfortable living on the savings they had accumulated) and the decline of the threat of Soekarno of neighbouring Indonesia for whom Lee wanted the British to stay. The connection between the two can also be seen without the threat disapplearing the expansion of the economy would not have been possible.

The inevitable question remains: If free elections are not possible and also advisable who calls the shots in the country and whose writ runs. India being a big country the experiment may not be successful and perhaps may not be tried at all. Perhaps the thought might prevail that the present situation has gone too far to be retrieved if at all. The extent of media freedom and the freedom to elect one's chosen representative has, in fact, gone too far and some may find it too late to recall it.

These are difficult questions and it may be really difficult to answer them. That Singapore is a small compact country goes without saying and similarly that India is a vast country, not easily susceptible to argument also goes without saying. But are we also conniving at the media's unlimited power, uncorrected by either the revealing comments, among others, of friend of the media who wants them to perform rather than take shelter at unbecoming things or the frank comments of a vast number of impartial observersr? That this power requires to be curbed is as clear as daylight.

If the unlimited power of the media is not restrained and if curbs are not put on it, a day might come, sooner rather than later, when the "wise" men and women may be asked to run the country. Their own clients prefer a regime under proper control, rather than the unlimited exhibition media power. So, a proper control on the media may be necessary in their own interest because the media are controlled by money-making tycoons and a regime under the thumb of the media may mean a regime of tycoons. Are we conscious of it and are we choosing it?

The success of some in the print media and some in the electronic media may only mean a success of business efficiency and rather than a success of the media power. The reasons for the efficiency output have been explained at relevant places and need not be gone into again. The makers of the success need not pat themselves on the back for it nor should they think that because of their wrong policy the success comes or people are subscribing to the particular paper or watching a particular channel.

Whether the Singapore model held up before the readers should be accepted or not is an open question. The time may have come, however, when the unlimited power of the media has to be curbed.

Notes and References

1. "Advani puts blame on media", *The Times of India,* Delhi, p. 5, single column top, on April 7, 2002.

Index